On the
Fringe

ON THE FRINGE

The Dispossessed in America

by

HENRY MILLER

Lexington Books

D.C. Heath and Company • *Lexington, Massachusetts* • *Toronto*

Library of Congress Cataloging-in-Publication Data
Miller, Henry, 1929–
On the fringe : the dispossessed in America / by Henry Miller.
p.   cm.
Includes bibliographical references (p.   ) and index.
ISBN 0-669-24905-X
1. Marginality, Social—United States—History. 2. Socially handicapped—United
States—History. 3. Outlaws—United States—History. 4. Subculture—History.
5. Outcasts—History. 6. Homelessness—United States—History. I. Title.
HN90.M26M55   1991
305.5'68'0973—dc20   90-13551
                                                                                                        CIP

Published simultaneously in Canada
Printed in the United States of America
International Standard Book Number: 0-669-24905-X
Library of Congress Catalog Card Number: 90–13551

The paper used in this publication meets the minimum requirements of
American National Standard for Information Sciences—Permanence
of Paper for Printed Library Materials, ANSI Z39.48-1984.

Year and number of this printing:

91 92 93 94 95 8 7 6 5 4 3 2 1

To Philipp, Laura, Charles, Adam, and—especially—Connie.

Contents

Acknowledgments

THIS book had its true inception many years before home-lessness became a topical social problem. Way back during the heyday of the hippies, staff members of the Haight-Ashbury Research Project and, especially, its irrepressible project director, Stephen Pittel, sparked my interest in the nomadic qualities of the young people of the 1960s. Ten years later, James Baumohl, a student of mine, reawakened my concern with the folks on the street. To Stephen and Jim, I gratefully acknowledge my in-debtedness; they put me on the path that led to writing *On the Fringe*.

I started work on this book, but then put it aside for a long time. Two colleagues in the School of Social Welfare prodded, cajoled, and nagged me so that I was finally forced to return to my writing and finish the book. To my friend Harry Specht, I am grateful for his moral support and encouragement, as well as for his push. Neil Gilbert—with whom I disagree about almost everything including the comprehension of homelessness—was also supportive even while he shoved me, a rather neat trick that only he could pull off. Thank you, Harry and Neil.

Many others had a hand in this work; my students scurried about finding sources, reading, commenting, and criticizing. Among the small army who did such things over the years I am especially grateful to Denise Burnette, Jane Holschuh, and Chris-tine Saulnier.

Finally, I thank my family. This is done not merely for the sake of form or domestic tranquility. Charles has nagged me about finishing this book for a long time; Adam, too, has pressured me, but through the telling way of silence. Philipp and Laura enthuse about whatever I do. My wife, Connie, has put up with a lot of moaning and groaning all the while remaining steadfast and confident. Bless you, all!

Introduction

OUTCASTS, misfits, loners, drifters—the social history of Western civilization is full of men, women, and children who fall outside the pale of convention by virtue of a feeble attachment to hearth and home. Six hundred and fifty years ago, when England still had forests, the homeless person was often called a valiant beggar, a "staff-striker," or a "rogue forlorn." Later, after the great voyages of discovery, during the age of colonization, the dispossessed often became pirates. At all times and in all places, we can find the outlaw and, among women, the prostitute.

The American experience sometimes produced heroic misfits: the mountain men; adventurous forty-niners always on the scent of a big strike; buffalo hunters; keelboat men; loggers; steel-driving railroad workers; and the quintessential American romantic figure, forever stoic in his solitude: the cowboy. Relatively few misfits, though, achieved heroic stature. For the most part, he or she was a figure usually despised and shunned. Hidden by the shadow of the mythic cowboy was the reality of the tramp or the drifter. And the heroic forty-niner, if examined closely, would often turn out to be a bum looking for easy riches.

The hallmarks of these people were ignorance, disease, unhappiness, and poverty. They were misfits because they lived on the edge of things; they could not "make it" by conventional means, so they did what society's "losers" have always done: they scrounged, hustled, stole, begged, connived, and sometimes even worked, and made do as best they could, and they lived wherever they could find shelter. Call them what you will—vagrants, tramps, hoboes, street people, or the homeless—every society in every age has had its share of people who live on the margins of conventional life.

Today the homeless have burst upon the consciousness of America. Hardly a day passes when the plight of people living without apparent shelter is not portrayed in the nation's press or when the television anchormen and anchorwomen do not mention the sad plight of people without homes. Public officials promise solutions, legislators conduct hearings, advocates harangue, and the more fortunate citizenry donate food, clothing, and money, but the problem of homelessness refuses to go away.

Homelessness is an ancient phenomenon. Indeed, the problem of significant numbers of people living without the benefit of a fixed home has been a feature of Western society at least since the later stages of feudalism and probably long before. Can we better comprehend the homeless in the United States of 1990 within the context of their ancestors? Does the sleeping figure on the subway grate have much in common with the hobo or the cowboy or, for that matter, with the poacher of Sherwood Forest? What is "the problem" all about?

On the Fringe was written to address these questions. It is a book about the disaffiliated, wandering, unsheltered folk of times past as well as times present. A newly visible generation of homeless has excited the sympathies of Americans, largely because many Americans believed that homeless people had long passed from the face of the United States. My book places the problem of homelessness within a historical context, but the people I will be discussing are not anachronistic remains. Indeed, I believe that the homeless population is resurgent and large and likely to grow even larger. The homeless have become a very visible population: the new American vagrant can be found in the urban metropolis, in neighborhoods peripheral to most of the major university campuses of this country, in the suburbs, and in rural areas.

But I am getting ahead of myself. I intend to address the problem of homelessness within a historical context. I will review the history of the vagrant in the Old World, specifically in England—when the vagrant or homeless person was called "a sturdy beggar." I will then examine the vagrant's life in America during the period between colonization and the Great Depression. My book's structure is not intended as a ritualistic obeisance to academic niceties. The requirements of scholarly form aside, there *is* something to be learned from the long history during which our English and American ancestors—and perhaps all civilizations—have attempted to cope with vagabonding and homeless men and women. The homeless crop up with disquieting frequency, but, as I hope to show, with *predictable* frequency; this is the intent of my historical chapters. I will then discuss vagrancy during the Great Depression, hippies, street people, and today's homeless.

Within a few paragraphs, I have used a handful of terms more or less synonymously: "valiant beggar," "misfit," "vagrant," "tramp," "hobo," "the homeless." As my book progresses other terms will be introduced to describe one or another class of homeless people, for the lexicon of homelessness is quite rich. Its very size stands as evidence of the historical and contemporary homeless problem: trivial events do not require such a large and varied vocabulary. I have deliberately chosen to refer to the ancestors of today's homeless in the vocabulary used by their own contemporaries. I have made little attempt to differentiate the fine distinctions between one term and another. Hopefully the narrative, as it unfolds, will clarify differences in terminology.

Society has been torn in the way it sees the unsettled or the wanderer; its ambivalence is painfully obvious. On the one hand, the vagrant is viewed as an enemy, a disrupter, a menace to established order, a parasite—he or she is someone to be shunned, stigmatized, or even killed. The vagrant of sixteenth-century England could be branded, imprisoned, or put to death. But the vagrant is also celebrated; he or she is sometimes perceived as the embodiment of all that is good in mankind. The holy wanderer who forsakes material comfort in the pursuit of spiritual fulfillment is beatified and canonized, like Saint Francis of Assisi. And the vagrant is romanticized as a vagabonding, unfettered, free spirit. In Walt Whitman's words, "Afoot and light-hearted, I take to the open road,/ Healthy, free, the world before me,/ The long brown path before me, leading wherever I choose."[1]

The literature on vagrancy and hoboism is overwhelming and partisan. It is almost impossible to find an authority who is not either repelled by or enamored of vagrant life.[2] The former stance is the most frequent among scholars, who tend to objectify vagrancy. Many are well intentioned; they see through the sentimentality and perceive what is a harsh reality: cold, hunger, illness, and harassment. The hobo is not a hearty soul, strong of body and hale of heart; he is likely to be tubercular and syphilitic. The well-intentioned viewer sees an object to be rehabilitated: the hobo is a victim of his own way of life. Another school of objectifiers is less sympathetic. In their eyes, the vagrant is a threat, a parasite who lives off of the labors of good citizens. The vagrant is one with beggars and prostitutes, highwaymen and bandits, conmen and hustlers—those deviant social elements who must be controlled, limited, and otherwise quarantined from the body social.

Poets, novelists, theologians, and journalists have a tendency to romanticize the vagrant life. Often they themselves are former adventurers who have "made it" and who in carefully expurgated memoirs sing of the soaring soul that comes from freedom.[3] The romantic believes that it is man's nature to be free. Vagrancy for the romantic is a symptom of this nature—or, conversely, a symptom of a social order and materialism that constrained freedom. Phillip O'Connor, one of the more recent apologists for wandering men, says it well: "Vagrants hold up the mirror to unnature."[4] That is the essence of the romantic argument.

Whether the approach to the vagrant be corrective, as represented by officialdom, or appreciative, as represented by the poets, what both perspectives hold in common is a presumption of choice. Somehow, it is assumed, the wanderer *chooses* his or her vagrant life. Nels Anderson, an authority on the American hobo, was more insightful. He may not have been the first, but he was the more persuasive of those who saw in hoboism the workings of vast social mechanisms—in particular, those related to labor and its position in the marketplace. Stripped of both his condemnation by the forces of the conservative establishment and his praise by the forces of romantic revolution, the hobo was first and foremost a migratory laborer. He worked—in special places and under special conditions—but nonetheless he was intimately tied to the vacillations of a much wider economic network. Anderson, however, was concerned with a hobo of a special kind: the solitary migratory male of the United States who, from the end of the Civil War to the beginning of World War I, made a singular and perhaps indispensable contribution to the development of the American West.

As we shall see, there were very special conditions operative in the social context during those years—conditions that had no exact counterpart in Medieval Europe, nor during the Great Depression, nor, surely, in our America of the last twenty years. Is it reasonable to extend Anderson's argument back into time— and forward as well—and hold to a theory of hoboism and vagrancy that rests ultimately on the vicissitudes of the labor force? Yes, with some qualification, I do believe that hoboism is an artifact of social events.

The requirements of the market determine not only the magnitude of the needed labor force but also the kinds of labor that are needed. There are times when a highly mobile labor force is essential. One such time occurred in England after the Black Death, another occurred in post–Civil War America. Both periods produced transient men and women: the first spawned England's vagrant, the second, America's hobo. Those were boom times; they could accommodate large numbers of unskilled workmen as well as workers with highly specialized skills. But there are other times when the labor market becomes glutted: too many hands compete for too few tasks. Such periods produce multitudes of wandering and homeless men and women. The depression of the 1930s was one such time. I will argue that the street people of the 1970s and the homeless people of today are also victims of a glutted labor market. *When labor began to take on the nature of a marketable commodity, vagrancy began to take on the forms that make it familiar to Western society.* When times are tough, the problem increases. To paraphrase the insight of a former attorney general of the United States: "When the going gets tough, those who find it tough get going." But when times are exceptionally good—I might add—the good, too, get going.

A time of economic expansion and of explosive opportunity generates large populations of moving people. They are *going* somewhere in response to news about opportunities for work, or for better work. They may even have money in their pockets; probably not very much, but enough, they hope, to carry them on their journey and tide them over until they have reached their destiny and rejoined the labor force. Alas, often the hoped-for opportunities don't exist. The hobo, and those like him who came before and after, was essentially a creature of an expanding and mobile labor force. The vagrant, on the other hand, is born of hard times. Driven by desperation and hope, he or she takes to the road.

The response of officialdom to the vagrant has always been relentlessly punitive. Historically, he or she has been treated as an object to be controlled when unwanted and exploited when needed. The literature on the vagrant never fails to emphasize his and her defects. So dedicated and meticulous an observer as Henry Mayhew, in his classic study, *London Labour and the London Poor* (1861–62), devotes four volumes to describing the sad lives of Victorian England's vagrants and outcasts.[5] The street people of London *were* a troublesome lot for the authorities to handle. They were poor, their employment opportunities were limited, and they were quite contemptuous of established society.

Society condemns the vagrant, but does the vagrant return this contempt? Vagrants are often ambivalent concerning their potential to leave the vagrant life behind them and become members of respectable society. The data concerning this issue are hideously one-sided, at least up until modern times. The record of vagrancy was written by the pens of the establishment: ministers of the king, bailiffs and sheriffs and justices of the peace, lawyers, and legislators, government committees, managers of poorhouses, workhouses, and asylums. Their descriptions and opinions represent the establishment's point of view. The vagabonds of Elizabethan England did not leave memoirs; when they did speak and when their speech was recorded it was usually in a courtroom. But when we come to recent times and have the opportunity to hear the voices of vagrant men speaking without duress, a note of sullen and even prideful contempt emerges:

> *The bum on the rod is a social flea*
> *Who gets an occasional bite,*
> *The bum on the plush is a social leech,*
> *Blood-sucking day and night.*

The bum on the rod is a load so light
That his weight we scarcely feel,
But it takes the labor of dozens of men
To furnish the other a meal.[6]

A mild note of penitence in this verse is surely overshadowed by a stronger theme of resentment. As social analysis, it is critical of an establishment that holds the vagrant in such contempt; we will find even more telling commentaries from the mouths of the street people of the 1970s.

In any event, even though the vagrant can best be viewed as a victim of a capricious and unfeeling labor market, it is impossible to ignore this other motif. He or she was also a misfit of sorts. Sometimes the vagrant didn't fit in because of a perversity of psychic structure or of very real deficits in personality and social skills. Moreover, the establishment was often correct: when the numbers of vagrants grew large, they could become a political danger.

Medieval Europe knew its share of transient people. The pilgrim served his God by trekking. Sometimes the pilgrim traveled hundreds or even thousands of miles. The Crusades left in their wake large numbers of displaced and wandering souls who were no longer attached to what they had left behind so many years before. But mostly, the social life of Europe was one of rather stable attachment of serf to manor. And then came a cataclysm that devastated the continent and hastened the end of an already decaying feudalism.

The plague of 1348 beggars the imagination. Between one-third and one-half of the population of Western Europe died within the span of two and one-half years.[7] The plague inspired terror and a frenzied flight; it also left as a legacy an immense shortage of labor. Manorial lords, those that were left after the Black Death, could not contain their serfs and freemen whose labor had now become such a sought-after necessity. England was overrun with wandering men. Stunned by the decimation of their families and the convulsion of their previously ordered lives, these people were easily lured away from their historic locale by higher wages and new possibilities. Inflation was rampant, the manors were in disrepair, and the men of privilege and power would not let these events go unchecked.

Thus, there appeared the first of what was to be a long series of measures—devised now by the landed classes and later by the men of capital—intended to harness and control the labor of men: The Statute of Laborers (1351). Edward III and his council enacted this ordinance to limit the movement of "idle" men; it was to become a prototype of the vagrancy laws passed over the centuries, and transported across the ocean to the new colonies in America to become the basis for vagrancy law in our fifty states.

England has been virtually possessed by the vagrancy "problem"—and with reason. A series of momentous and cyclical events occurring over six centuries have served to loosen the ties that bind men to permanency and stability. The enclosure movement helped to change the English from a rural, farming population to an urban, manufacturing population in the course of two centuries. The enclosure movement also produced enormous disruption, a new kind of mass poverty, and armies of vagrants and mendicants. The growth of cities created another kind of poverty; a never-ending series of wars left behind ever-recurring cohorts of the homeless. Thus, the legacy of change: beggars, highwaymen, soldiers, seamen, sneaks, smugglers, prostitutes, mudlarks, pirates, pickpockets—a parade of marginal, disaffiliated men and women.

Many of the disaffiliated crossed the ocean and came to America; indeed, some would say they founded and made America. The conquistadors were not the finest men of Spain; their ranks were filled with misfits, scoundrels, criminals, and the ragged edge of the nobility. Not all the early settlers of New England were Pilgrims, Puritans, and other kinds of religious dissidents. Many were the flotsam of an English society strained by religious fratricide, civil war, and rapid economic change. England deliberately shipped many of its vagrants, petty criminals, and outcasts to America. The Puritans brought with them English Poor Law, with its special codicils directed at begging and vagrancy. But the vagrant was a vagrant only so long as he or she stayed in town; if vagrant people took off for Kentucky or Ohio, they became something else: pioneers, perhaps settlers.

The Civil War brought social disruption to both North and South, but in the South it undermined the aristocracy and ended slavery. But the Civil War was a godsend for the West. Western exploitation and growth created a need for men—all kinds of men; men to work the mines, and log, and punch cows, and reap crops, and build railroads—200,000 miles of railroads. Here was born Nels Anderson's hobo, the migratory worker with his bindle, who worked in a mine or on a railroad gang or gathered crops for a few weeks or months, built up a stake for one huge and extravagant spree, and then set off again for another round of work. This man was a creature of the need for mobile labor; unattached labor, rugged labor to be done in rugged places. He may have been much like that survivor of the Black Death five hundred years earlier. He was a man who could call his own shots and the sheriff be damned.

When the West was won, when the railroads were built and the mines dug out, when McCormick's harvester replaced dozens of laborers, and when the open range was finally fenced, the hobo—as Anderson knew him—began to disappear. He "retired" as it were—to West Madison St. in Chicago, South of Mission in San Francisco, the Bowery in New York. Thus were born the skid rows of America. The hobo became a bum, a man alone and unemployed with only the possibility of cheap wine to keep him going and the myth of "the free spirit" to warm his soul.

From the first decade of the twentieth century until the Great Depression, the hobo was a fading phenomenon. But, as has happened so many times before in Western history, another event came along to resurrect the solitary transient. The crash of 1929 was another one of those catastrophes that created multitudes of vagrant men, women, and children. This time, however, there was no work at the end of the line. The problem of homeless people was so great during the early years of the 1930s that there arose a special organ of government to deal with the crisis: the Federal Transients Bureau. The problem was alleviated somewhat by the passage of the Federal Emergency Relief and Social Security acts. And then came World War II and an economic boom. The army and industry began to absorb the rootless multitudes. Once again vagrancy disappeared from public view—until the 1960s with its hippies, the 1970s with the street people, and the 1980s with "the homeless."

Despite appearances, what follows is not a history of vagrancy and homelessness. Someday, hopefully, a competent historian will write that history. This book is not even a history of the *idea* of such phenomena. Rather, it is more like a history of the *polemic* that has raged about the homeless person wherever he or she has been found. The polemic derives from the persistent assumption that homeless people are morally deficient. The counterargument, feeble in comparison to the numbers of voices raised against the homeless over the centuries, provides the other side of the polemic. It is that the homeless, simply, are poor people who cannot purchase shelter.

It is in this context that I must declare what kind of wandering I will not consider—a set of exclusions—a rough typology of people who, for the most part, are rarely included among current and past considerations of the homeless.

There are, first, the true *migratories,* most from the darkness of undocumented history. The people of Asia who crossed the Bering Straits to populate the Americas and ultimately formed Incan and Aztec civilizations; the incredible voyagers of Oceania who settled Tahiti, Hawaii, and Easter Island; the great migrations of Aryans, Huns, and Mongols; the movements of Picts, Jutes, Celts, Angles, Saxons, Danes, and Normans who settled Britain—all these different groups form a class of people who surely were homeless, at least for a time, by technical standards. But, whatever such heroic feats were all about, they represent another and intuitively different form of residential tenuousness.

Then there are *nomads:* Bedouin, the Eskimo, the aborigine of Australia, the Masai of East Africa, the Indian tribes of America's plains, and other such hunters, gatherers, and herders who are rarely perceived as vagrants or beggars or homeless. Obviously, such peoples are, by the nature of their own culture and economy, geographically mobile. For contemporary domesticated man to view nomads as homeless would be as illogical as to see very young children as unemployed. Nomads are not *supposed* to be residentially stable. One curious exception is the Gypsies, a people who were and still are a source of much bother to the burghers of Europe and even to some communities of 20th-century America. But the Gypsy is a very special and complicated case and is best left outside the bounds of this study.

And there are *slaves*. Human history is a sad record of the enslavements of whole peoples. The enforced exodus of blacks from the continent of Africa to the Americas is the classic case of this type, but there have been many other enslavements. This class of uprooted and homeless is again a special case. But when the slave ran away, as in the Europe of the Dark Ages, to lose himself among the larger group of vagrants, his status as a special case begins to get fuzzy.

Refugees comprise another exclusion. The displacements of peoples by the scourges of war, persecution, or political upheaval form another special class. I have in mind such tragic events as the vast transfer of populations that occurred between India and Pakistan in the late 1940s; the merciless expulsion of Armenians from their ancient homelands by the Turks; the diaspora of the Jews; the exodus of the Palestinians; the flight of the "boat people" from Vietnam—a long and bitter inventory of such events can be generated. Among these, of course, are the movements of peoples who flee from the approach, and sometimes the withdrawal, of vast armies. Uprooted either by force or by fear, the refugee is someone who would have stayed with his or her home if he or she could.

Survivors are similar to what Alexander Vexliard calls "elementary vagrants."[8] They are closely akin to refugees but in this instance the source of the disrupting event is nature herself. Floods, earthquakes, hurricanes, fires, and famines represent the more typical disasters. The unfortunate victims of these occasions are, again, a special but by no means trivial type. Usually the response of officialdom to such homeless is benign and even helpful—a response that is atypical for the agents of convention.

In spite of the ambiguities that sometimes occur, it is apparent that the above groups of people are not what most people have in mind, today, when they think of the homeless. Indeed, it is not what most people had in mind of old when they thought of vagrants or hoboes or valiant beggars or sturdy beggars. From a strictly formal point of view, members of the groups were surely transient and they were obviously homeless, at least for a time. But they have always been conceived of as special cases worthy of exclusion from the more pressing category of concern. The rationale for the exclusion is obvious: these groups of people lacked two of the essential conditions for being considered among the vagrant homeless.

First, they were usually clear victims of powerful forces outside of their control. Second, and this is most important, they could not a priori be presumed to have any kind of individual deficit, whether it be moral, physical, or psychological. The dual criteria of *nonvictimization* and *individual deficit* have been the critical definitional characteristics of vagrancy throughout history. I will return to these ideas later in this book.

In any event, this is primarily a book about the *unattached* wanderer, and more exactly the unattached wanderer of the Western world. There are such people in the East; India has its beggars—as did China. Indeed, there is a long tradition of mendicancy in the Orient. But my inquiry had to have some boundaries and I preferred to draw the line around the Western hobo and vagrant, forebears and antecedents.

On the
Fringe

1

On Beggars, Vagabonds, Highwaymen, and Vagrants:

The Legacy of Social Disorder

T HE continent of Europe entered the fourteenth century with a rather rich history of social discord upon which to build. Imperial Rome, of course, had come and long since gone; successive waves of barbarians had swept across Europe, had settled, and had taken on a thin facade of civilization. Wars were frequent and brutal. Famine occurred periodically. Migrations of whole peoples often took place; Britain alone suffered a succession of invasions and none-too-pleasant settlements by Jutes, Angles, Saxons, Danes, Norsemen, and finally Normans. Chaos and disruption were all too frequent—even endemic. Society's recurrent turbulence caused many people to become detached from whatever stability they had attained. Soldiers, when their campaign was over and their soldiering finished, often returned home to discover that their homes and villages had disappeared. The Crusades, extending over many decades, left in their wake many idle hands; years of looting, pillaging, and fighting through the Eastern Roman Empire and in the Holy Land did not prepare men for an easy readjustment to civilian life. Some returning Crusaders brought with them leprosy: the outcast leper was to be a feature of the European landscape for several centuries. Banditry and robbery were not unusual careers for returning

Crusaders. Robin Hood, if he lived at all, may well have been a disaffected former soldier or Crusader. The forests, heaths, and waste places of England harbored many strange and sometimes dangerous people—most of whom, unlike the legendary bandit of Sherwood Forest, cared not a whit for the well-being of the poor peasant.

Many slaves who were manumitted won freedom but lost their homes. Some slaves became free men without the sanction of the legal process. Movement, in the form of flight, was an intelligent solution to a condition of bondage. Some men of the holy orders emulated the sanctity of Jesus and his Apostles, took their vows of poverty seriously, and walked the roads preaching and begging for their meals and lodgings. The mendicant friar was a fixture of the medieval countryside. So too were the students of Oxford; begging was a common, indeed, an expected source of support for students and, on occasion, for their teachers.[1] Troubadours, ballad mongers, minstrels, and players moved from town to town plying their entertainments and spreading the news of the day. Pilgrims, too, in great numbers, took to the road.

Vagrancy, as a defined crime, did not yet exist. Indeed, during the High Middle Ages there was a tendency to idealize mendicant poverty; the exemplar, of course, was Saint Francis and his brothers who wandered the realm wrapped in an aura of divine approval. The Franciscan ideal of a sacred and holy poverty did not long prevail; even within the lifetime of the saint, the Franciscan order accumulated considerable wealth. The Catholic church, though it glorified the ideal of a holy mendicancy, never managed to cope with its reality when practiced by Franciscans and others. The glorification and, often, the sanctification of vagrant mendicancy was to return, nonetheless, to Western consciousness from time to time; to this day it forms an important kernel of the romantic argument for vagrant life. Outside of the recurrent struggles within the church in this respect, there were and continue to be various antinomian movements that hold materialism to be an abomination. The Diggers of Stuart times were an approximation to such an ideal. Their namesakes in San Francisco's Haight-Ashbury district, during the heyday of our own hippie experience in the 1960s, were, perhaps, an even closer example of the model of a holy and self-imposed poverty.

In any event, in the Middle Ages it had not yet become a crime to be poor and rootless. Strangers, notwithstanding religious injunctions to be charitable, were not necessarily well received by settled folk. Anyone who undertook a journey may have feared that cutthroats and bandits lurked behind every bush. Fugitives—whether slave or free—were hunted down. But the vagrant was not an object of control and repression. The linkage of vagrancy with pauperism and welfare law remained for future generations. To be a vagrant in the fourteenth century was not criminal nor was it even perceived as improper. The folk hero of our childhood fairy tales, the youngest son who leaves his father's nest to seek his fortune or otherwise make his way in the world, is based on the reality of the times. There were many young men, even in the days when the kingdom was relatively stable, who were faced with the problems caused by primogeniture, the system of inheritance that dictated that the eldest son inherited all his father's land. If a younger son couldn't find a wife who owned land, he had only a few other choices: work for his brother, join the army or the church, or take to the open road.

By the start of the fourteenth century medieval life was beginning to show strains. But first we need to see how it appeared before the cracks grew ever larger and before the entire edifice of feudalism collapsed. The medieval village has been aptly characterized as

[self-sufficient] in its labour and its poverty; often suffering from famine but never from unemployment; little connected with the world beyond its forest bounds, except through the personal activities and requirements of its lord; supplying its own simple needs; containing its own miller, craftsman, and spinsters; feeding itself by tilling, on traditional methods, the strips owned by villeins in the open field, and by sharing the common rights over meadow and waste. . . . the village was "a manor" held by some lord, resident or non-resident, lay or spiritual. . . . [The manor consisted of the] lord and his villeins, who composed the great majority of the village, and by whose compulsory labour his domain was tilled under the supervision of his bailiff.[2]

This system prevailed, with some variation, over most of feudal Europe. It began to come apart, slowly, with the rise of free men; the magnetic attraction of towns; the first trivial nucleus of a middle class; an important—and in those days—rather unmanageable rise in population; and a series of bad harvests. Then came the cataclysm that was the Black Death.

No account of this pestilence matches the vivid description of Boccaccio in his introduction to *The Decameron*. Here he offers a glimpse into hell.

> The sum of thirteen hundred and forty-eight years had elapsed since the fruitful Incarnation of the Son of God, when the noble city of Florence, which for its great beauty excels all others in Italy, was visited by the deadly pestilence. . . .
>
> For in the early spring of the year we have mentioned, the Plague began, in a terrifying and extraordinary manner, to make its disastrous effects apparent. . . .
>
> Some people were of the opinion that a sober and abstemious mode of living considerably reduced the risk of infection. They therefore formed themselves into groups and lived in isolation from everyone else. Having withdrawn to a comfortable abode where there were no sick persons, they locked themselves in and settled down to a peaceable existence, consuming modest quantities of delicate foods and precious wines and avoiding all excesses. They refrained from speaking to outsiders, refused to receive news of the dead or the sick, and entertained themselves with music and whatever other amusements they were able to devise. . . .
>
> Others took the opposite view, and maintained that an infallible way of warding off this appalling evil was to drink heavily, enjoy life to the full, go round singing and merrymaking, gratify all of one's cravings whenever the opportunity offered, and shrug the whole thing off as one enormous joke. Moreover, they practiced what they preached to the best of their ability, for they would visit one tavern after another, drinking all day and night to immoderate excess. . . .
>
> Some people, pursuing what was possibly the safer alternative, callously maintained that there was no better or more

efficacious remedy against a plague than to run away from it. Swayed by this argument, and sparing no thought for anyone but themselves, large numbers of men and women abandoned their city, their homes, their relatives, their estates and their belongings, and headed for the countryside, either in Florentine territory or, better still, abroad. . . .

. . . this scourge had implanted so great a terror in the hearts of men and women that brothers abandoned brothers, uncles, their nephews, sisters, their brothers, and in many cases wives deserted their husbands. . . .

. . . In the fortified towns, conditions were similar to those in the city itself on a minor scale; but in the scattered hamlets and countryside proper, the poor unfortunate peasants and their families had no physicians or servants whatever to assist them, and collapsed by the wayside, in their fields, and in their cottages at all hours of the day and night, dying more like animals than human beings. Like the townspeople, they too grew apathetic in their possessions. Moreover they all behaved as though each day was to be their last, and far from making provision for the future by tilling their lands, tending their flocks, and adding to their previous labours, they tried in every way they could think of to squander the assets already in their possession. . . .

Ah, how great a number of splendid palaces, fine houses, and noble dwellings, once filled with retainers, with lords and with ladies, were bereft of all who had lived there, down to the tiniest child! How numerous were the famous families, the vast estates, the notable fortunes, that were seen to be left without a rightful successor! How many gallant gentlemen, fair ladies, and sprightly youths, who would have been judged hale and hearty by Galen, Hippocrates and Aesculapius (to say nothing of others), having breakfasted in the morning with their kinsfolk, acquaintances and friends, supped that same evening with their ancestors in the next world![3]

This scourge, so graphically depicted by Boccaccio, arrived in Sicily in October 1347; by the spring of 1348 it had spread through all of Italy, most of France, and the southeast of Spain; in the winter of 1348 it appeared in Bristol, England, and within another year had infected the remainder of that kingdom and all of Europe. How many died? Philip Ziegler offers a conservative estimate: "As a rough and ready rule of thumb . . . , the statement that a third of the population died of the Black Death should not be too misleading. The figure might quite easily be as high as 40 percent or as low as 30 percent."[4]

Whether the toll was one in three or one in two, such a calamity could not fail to result in a severe dislocation of social structure and economy. Feudalism was done for—it was probably done for anyway, but the plague in a period of months forever changed the traditional bond of man to his lord and to his land. As G. M. Trevelyan aptly stated, the plague and its immediate consequences "precipitated the class struggle, and embittered the process of emancipating the villein."[5] The plague killed so many people that it created a labor shortage and undermined all the traditional ties that bound the agricultural worker to his lord's estate. Those who managed to survive the plague—whether freemen, serfs, or slaves—often recognized that they could flee their former master and manor and negotiate better terms with a new master elsewhere, with little fear of reprisal. Landlords who were slow to make concessions to tenants might soon discover that once-faithful servants had disappeared. After all, there were plenty of landowners in neighboring areas eager and willing to take on new hands—and no questions asked about previous status. Further, towns were beginning to emerge. They were a far cry from anything that we moderns would call cities, nonetheless populations of people were beginning to coalesce around manufacturing and distribution hubs. The cloth trade was growing; for those who were tired of the farms altogether there was the intriguing possibility of a radically new industry located, sometimes, in these nascent cities.

Things could not continue without some attempt to maintain the old order by those affronted by a free and mobile labor force. For the landed nobility the terror of the recent plague was quickly overshadowed by their fear of the loss of ancient privilege. The Statute of Laborers, enacted in 1351, was a device to keep workers from transferring their labor from one employer to another.[6] This remarkable document contains within it the official analysis of the malady: mobile wage labor was a function of individual perversity or roguery. This insight from officialdom stubbornly refused to die as the centuries unfolded. The Statute of Laborers was portentous of other things to come both in terms of attitudes and legislation:

> Because a great part of the people, and especially of workmen and servants, late died of the pestilence, many seeing the necessity of masters and great scarcity of servants, will not serve unless they may receive excessive wages, and some rather willing to beg in idleness than by labour to get their living; We, considering the grievous incommodities which of the lack especially of ploughmen and such labourers may hereafter come, have upon deliberation and treaty with the prelates and nobles, and learned men assisting us, of their mutual consent ordained:
>
> That every man and woman of our realm of England, of what condition he be, free or bond, able in body, and within the age of threescore years, not living in merchandise, nor exercising any craft, nor having of his own whereof he may live, nor proper land, about whose tillage he may himself occupy, and not serving any other, if he in convenient service (his estate considered) be required to serve, he shall be bounden to serve him which so shall him require; And take only the wages, livery, need, or salary which were accustomed to be given in the places where he oweth to serve, the XX year of our reign of England, or five or six other common years next before. Provided always, that the lords be preferred before others in their bondmen or their land tenants, so in their service to be retained: so that nevertheless the said lords shall retain no more than be necessary for them; And if any such man or woman, being so required to serve, will not the same do, that proved by two true men before the sheriff or the bailiff be done, he shall anon be taken by them, or any of them, and committed to the next gaol, there to remain under strait keeping, till he find surety to serve in the form aforesaid.
>
> That if a workman or servant depart from service before the time agreed upon, he shall be imprisoned.
>
> That the old wages and no more shall be given to servants.
>
> That if the lord of a town or manor do offend against this statute in any point, he shall forfeit the treble value.
>
> That if any artificer or workman take more wages than were wont be paid, he shall be committed to the gaol.
>
> That victuals shall be sold at reasonable prices.
>
> Item, because that many valiant beggars, as long as they may live of begging, do refuse to labour, giving themselves to

idleness and vice, and sometime theft and other abominations; none upon the said pain of imprisonment shall, under the colour of pity or alms, give anything to such, which may labour, or presume to favour them towards their desires, so that thereby they may be compelled to labour for their necessary living.

That he that taketh more wages than is accustomably given, shall pay the surplusage to the town where he dwelleth, towards a payment to the King of a tenth or a fifteenth granted to him.[7]

Much could be said of this ordinance. It was intended, primarily, to control wages; indeed, it attempted to establish what would be called in current terminology a wage "rollback"—back to the twentieth year of Edward III's reign, 1347, the year just prior to the arrival of the terrible pestilence. The ordinance attempted to balance the rollback in wages with an attempt to hold down costs—"victuals shall be sold at reasonable prices"—but unfortunately, such price controls were not given more than incidental mention within the detail of the instrument.

More importantly, however, we see the seed of that awful distinction that was to haunt English Poor Law and American welfare law, for ever after: the distinction made between the able-bodied and what were later to be called the worthy poor.[8] This distinction had played no part in the giving of charity prior to the chaos precipitated by the Black Death. The Catholic church, the institutional center for charity enterprises, bestowed alms on *all* poor persons; the means test based on a person's need calculated according to his/her ability and willingness to work was an invention of incipient capitalism and not a product of ecclesiastical law. The reference in the statute to "idleness" was completely gratuitous; idleness was not a serious problem. The real problem was "moving on" to better wages; if idleness existed it was a characteristic of the lords and other landowners. Villeins and free men had plenty to do; indeed, too much in the way of work opportunity seemed to be the problem the framers of the statute were addressing.

The Statute of Laborers did not work. The Black Death was the straw that broke the back of the manorial system; for a while at least the scales were tipped against the landowner. Governmental action did not succeed in turning the clock backward. The legislation was less an instrument of reactionary change than a testimony to the reality of revolutionary changes: "the most radical of these changes was the new desire, even determination on the part of the medieval labourer to have a say in deciding his terms of employment and to seek his fortune elsewhere if such a right were denied him."[9] What the statute *did* do, however, was to initiate the long legal process that made free labor—and by implication, idle labor—a condition of some hazard and eventually of opprobrium. Vagrancy began to be seen as a threat to the order of things; in 1351 that order was feudalism. Much later, vagrancy was to be perceived as a threat to capitalism.

It soon became apparent to the onetime serf that free and mobile labor was not without its shortcomings. To be unconnected to land and without a clear means of subsistence had now become a crime. England—indeed, all of Europe—eventually made a remarkable recovery from the devastations of the plague. The birthrate soared and people took up their new lives. The attempt to control labor continued with a series of amendments and extensions to the statute of 1351; the struggle was intense as king and gentry tried desperately to retard the process of the emancipation of villeins, especially since the latter were unwilling to bend and return to the earlier way of life. The century, which saw the invention of the vagrant, culminated in the fierce drama of the Peasants Revolt which, at least by a loose interpretation, can be seen as the medieval version of the general strike. An army of angry peasants marched on London in 1381 to demand relief from high taxes. They beheaded the archbishop of Canterbury and besieged the king, Richard II, at the Tower of London. The king eventually promised redress of grievances and a free pardon for the rebels, but "Every promise made to the peasants in the hour of need was broken, and a bloody assize made mock of the pardons granted by the King."[10] But the march of history could not be changed and the English villein, over the course of the next several generations, won his freedom and his right to sell his own labor.

The next century was to portend the vicissitudes of the victory:

The fluidity of labour had come, altering the whole outlook of economic society. The change from the fixed and limited rights and duties of the serf to the competition and uncertainty of

the open labour market was by no means wholly to the labourer's advantage, though for a hundred years after the Black
Death the dearth of labour enabled him to command a high
price. But in the later part of the Fifteenth Century, when the
population had recovered, wages fell. Under the modern re-
gime, though famine was more rare and the average standard
of life was raised, the horrors of unemployment became known
and the "sturdy beggars" of Tudor times had little joy of their
freedom.[11]

The vagrancy of fifteenth- and sixteenth-century England
was not like that which had provoked the Statute of Laborers.
The official, governmental record reads as though the country
was overrun with freeloaders, idle men who with calculated malice and a disregard for the virtues of hard work would beg,
scrounge, rob, rape, and murder. There was, indeed, a long
series of unsettling events in those two centuries. The cloth trade
in fine fabric woven for sale to foreign markets—a skill derived
from Flemish immigrants in the fourteenth century—created a
new class of bourgeois with a very real stake in thrift and stability.
Certain "cloth towns" began to gain prominence, and London
itself became a very busy mercantile center.[12] The long Wars of
the Roses (1455–85) caused further social disruption and generated a large body of unemployed retainers and soldiers. Migrations from Ireland and Wales contributed to an already full
cauldron of disaffiliated people. And when Henry VIII broke
with Rome and closed the monasteries, a huge population of
dispossessed clergy added another element to unemployed
England.

Enclosure was, perhaps, the most disruptive process that
served to tear people from their already tenuous attachments.
The traditional open fields that many small farmers required
for their subsistence were "enclosed" by landowners, who wanted
this land for the pasturage of sheep to supply the cloth industry
with wool. Since the use of open fields held in common with
other village folk often provided the poor peasant with the margin of sustenance that meant the difference between having
enough to eat and starving, enclosure could mean death. Without
a share of the open fields to plant in or to use as pasture for the
family cow or a few sheep, many small farmers were forced to

take to the roads, where they became the "sturdy beggars," "staff-strikers," and "rogues forlorn" who figure so prominently in the literature and laws of Tudor times.[13]

New laws designed to eliminate vagrants and beggars were tough. An act passed during the reign of Edward VI in 1547 begins: "For as much as Idleness and Vagabonding is the mother and root of theft, robberies and all evil acts and other mischiefs . . . ,"[14] and then proceeds to ordain a variety of punitive measures:

> Every person not impotent and "loitering or wandering and not seeking work, *or leaving it when engaged*"[15] is to be apprehended and taken before a justice of the peace. He is then to be "marked with a hot iron in the breast [with] the mark of V." The unfortunate vagrant was then to become the slave of his captor.[16]

> The new slave was to be fed on bread and water and "such refuse meats as the master thinks fit." The period of enslavement was two years.

> If the slave ran away and was apprehended, he was to be beaten and "marked on the forehead or ball of the cheek with a hot iron with the sign of an S."

> A slave running away a second time was to suffer the pains of death as a felon.

This draconian act went on to provide further niceties for infant beggars and women, as well as special exemptions for legitimate travelers and legitimate beggars: cripples, lepers, students, and the like. The impotent poor, then, were intended to be exempted from the harsh penalties of the legislation. But intentions and realities often clashed—to the misfortune of the truly needy. The problem centered on definition: what characteristics identified the truly needy, and who made the final determination of "true" need versus "false" need. Obviously, such decisions were left to the local authorities, who thus had the power to condemn any undesirable as a vagrant—and often did.

The act, as might be expected, had little effect on the magnitude of the problem. Further enactments by industrious parliaments enlarged the scope of coverage to include "common players" (1549), "Tinkers and Peddlers" (1551), Gypsies (1553), and minstrels (1554). It is difficult to say how energetically these laws were enforced. Wallace claims that the number of vagrants who were apprehended for a third time and hanged was 12,000; this sounds excessive.[17] The problem, of course, was that the vagabondage addressed by the statutes was rampant. Tudor governments could not see that vagrancy was a function of the economic upheavals I mentioned earlier. It was, in effect, a problem of unemployment rather than "idleness." Most vagrants would have preferred to be working, but they couldn't find jobs. They begged to stay alive, not because they enjoyed begging.

One of the very few analyses of the problem by a contemporary supports this assertion. Thus a Mr. Stanley, a highway robber by default, wrote to King James early in the seventeenth century:

> I make no doubt (most gracious sovereign) but it is evident to all men, that Beggerie and Thieverie did never more abound within this your Realme of England, and the cause of this miserie is Idleness, and the only meanes to cure the same must be by his contrarie, which is Labour; for tell the begging Souldier, and the wandering and sturdy Beggar, that they are able to work for their living, and bid them go to work, they will presently answer you, *they would work if they could get it.* But if workhouses were set up in all great parishes, it will take away all such defensories and usual answers, and then it will be tryed whether they will work or not.[18]

Mr. Stanley could not have put it more clearly: "they would work if they could get it" and then he goes on to suggest a remedy that sounds familiar to contemporary ears: the equivalent of a public works program. Alas, the king did not listen to the highwayman. Vagrancy was officially viewed as a self-chosen career of idleness and unemployment as a moral rather than an economic condition.

Vagrancy persisted, and local authorities and Parliament were resolute in their determination to suppress it. The official record, at the turn of the seventeenth century, is full of complaints about laxity in the enforcement of the antivagrancy statutes—by now a compilation of law exquisite in detail and inclusiveness. Periodically cries of indignation were raised about how the laws were not being faithfully and responsibly executed by the proper officials. The times were tough; poverty was rampant and compounded by an influx into the Western counties of Irish paupers fleeing famine in Ireland. Indeed, starving beggars were so ubiquitous that in 1613 King James was constrained to mint new, smaller coins—the wretched farthing—for "relief to the poor as they will thereby receive small alms." Enclosure was proceeding at a rapid pace moderated not at all by the misgivings of some of the more fortunate and the antagonism of the displaced:

> *The law locks up the man or woman*
> *That steals the goose from off the common;*
> *But leaves the greater villain loose*
> *Who steals the common from the goose.*[19]

The transportation to the new American colonies of criminals during the seventeenth and eighteenth century provided some relief for the problem. The transportation of vagabonds began during the reign of Elizabeth I and reached a peak during the following several decades. As A. L. Beier tersely observes, "the whole business was of dubious legality" partly because most of the victims of such banishment were children or youths, rather than the hardened criminals and rogues defined by the statutes.[20] The unfortunate vagrant could be spirited off the streets and offered a choice: he, or sometimes she, could board a vessel for the Virginia or the Massachusetts Bay colonies, or be imprisoned as a felon. More often than not, the unhappy vagrant chose a term of indenture in the New World. The term of indenture in the colonies varied between two and seven years for adults; male children were bound until the age of twenty-one, and girls until their marriage. Their fate in America was far from rosy; of 165 children sent from the city of London to Virginia in 1619 few survived to adulthood. Many died on the overseas journey and at least five were killed by native Indians.

Some vagrants didn't wait to be arrested and then transported. The promoters and financial backers of the various colonial enterprises often advertised for settlers and paid the travel expenses of volunteers. Many vagrants chose this method of emigration. More probably would have volunteered, but England lacked enough ships to handle the potential demand.[21]

During harvest times in England vagrants seemed to mysteriously disappear. A proclamation of 1630 stated quite boldly that "harvest being ended, the former similar proclamation of the 23rd April last past is to be put in execution"[22]—which is to say that it was time to crack down again on the unemployed.

By now officials could not maintain legal distinctions among paupers, vagrants, and rogues. Some recognized no essential differences, while others tried to distinguish between "worthy" and "unworthy" beggars but were forced to rely on little more than intuition for help. What should have been obvious—and still is too often forgotten—is that all vagrant people are poor and that, in the absence of a welfare apparatus, many poor people become vagrant. The relationship between being poor and being vagrant derives from a rather simple fact: the inability to pay for shelter. Moreover, when suffering from hunger and desperation many poor people will become criminal: poverty breeds roguery.

It is worthwhile to note that the greater part of people who were apprehended under the vagrancy laws during these times were very young. Indeed, today we would think of them as children. Beier, in his scrutiny of documented hearings, concluded that 97 percent of the people arrested for vagrancy and examined by local constables were under age twenty-one and 54 percent were under the age of sixteen.[23] What these figures indicate about the integrity and cohesion of family life is left for the reader to determine; but there is plenty of anecdotal evidence to suggest that what we in the late twentieth century call "family dysfunction" is not a new phenomenon. Youth is a characteristic of vagrant populations. Picking up and going someplace, leaving all ties behind, is a more viable option for the young than for the old. Life on the road is hard. It requires health, strength, and the willingness to take risks—all characteristics of youth.

The legislative machinery for dealing with vagrancy had, for a long while, revolved around the concept of residency or "settlement": according to this idea, people were bound to the community of their previous residence and, ultimately, to the community of their origin for their social and economic identity, including any assistance in a time of need. Thus, a hapless vagrant arrested in London could—if he escaped prison, impressment, or transportation—be legally returned to his place of birth. His local community was charged with the responsibility of providing him with aid. This tradition was formalized in the 1662 Act of Settlement, provoked, in part, by masses of disbanded soldiers seeking work. The act authorized local authorities to send back to his last place of domicile any newcomer who seemed likely to become a public charge. In theory, and often practice, only people possessed of some means of support were legally free to move about and seek employment. The Settlement Act created laborers, in effect, who were "serfs without land." The linkage of public assistance with a person's community of origin became a major tenet of welfare thought. The system was transported to the United States in colonial times and it remained a central feature of this country's public charity until the recent civil rights movement when, in 1969, the Supreme Court struck down all residency requirements for public aid.

The last half of the seventeenth century continues the chronicle of a kingdom overrun with poor and vagrant men and, occasionally, women. The towns and cities were growing in size, the cloth industry became more and more important to the English economy, "masterless" men abounded, and highwaymen seemed to be everywhere. Concern renewed about able-bodied men and women who tried to pass themselves off as deserving poor folk.[24] A curious example of this anxiety is made manifest in a rather pathetic announcement to the good citizens of London by the authorities of Bethlehem Hospital that they *do not* issue identifying certificates or insignia to their freed lunatics. Evidently, some enterprising vagrants were wearing copper medallions as a badge of their madness in the hopes of extracting a few farthings from the unsuspecting. Caveat emptor!

It is important to emphasize again that the sorry vagabonds of these two centuries were primarily displaced workers in what was then a very unstructured and even chaotic labor force. Beier made a careful examination of records kept by the local officials of Chester, Leicester, Reading, and Warwick during the years

from 1571 to 1642. These officials, punctilious in their adherence
to law, were charged with examining accused vagrants. Beier
found that the vast majority of supposed vagrants were experienced in the job market.[25] Indeed, many were on their way to
some place of employment—or what they hoped would be a
place of employment—when they were apprehended by zealous
authorities. They worked, when they could, at legitimate jobs:
they were farm laborers, clothmakers, tinkers, petty chapmen
(peddlers), servants, soldiers, sailors, former apprentices or jour-
neymen who had lost their masters.

The decisive fact, though, was that in Tudor and Stuart England wage labor was often synonymous with poverty. In twen-
tieth-century America, we claim to have a very mobile labor force.
We pale, however, in comparison to the England of these earlier
centuries when the entire labor force was mobile. Working at
one regular job was out of the question except for those master
artisans who found a secure place in one of the exclusive guilds.
As Beier reminds us, working, vagabonding, and begging (and
probably petty crime) formed a continuum rather than a set of
discrete activities. "Any one vagabond, contrary to the literary
stereotypes of specialist rogues, might engage in all three activities, all on the same day, simply because he had to."[26] The Elizabethan underworld was a large and fluid body.

It was believed then, and it is still frequently claimed, that
the understratum of those times was formed into organized and
structured societies—brotherhoods of beggars or guilds of petty
criminals. For England, at least, this was simply not so. There
might be a very small kernel of fact to the allegation in respect
to the vagrants and beggars of continental Europe; a popular
literature does indeed exist on the beggar societies of Paris. Most
noteworthy is the folklore that evolved out of "the Court of
Miracles" in seventeenth-century Paris, so named because the
armies of cripples, blind, and disfigured—when they retired after
a day spent begging to the hovels of their night—would be mi-
raculously transformed into whole and healthy human beings.
The Parisian slum was a sinkhole of misery, of course, but the
myth of the beggar king holding court among his fellows with
everyone laughing at the gullibility of the good citizens was apparently too tempting a portrait to be left undrawn. Ideas con-

cerning secret societies of beggars and vagabonds are the stuff of pure romance. Tales about a hierarchy among happy-go-lucky free spirits carried over to this country and to the hoboes of America. We know that the idea of vagrants creating a secret society based on a monarchy, with a king, princes, ranks of nobles, etc., is complete nonsense and clearly the product of a romantic wish to transform harsh reality.[27] The romance persists, however, fed by such charming and artistic creations as *The Beggar's Opera* and *The Three-Penny Opera.*

The ingenuity of the kingdom's free laborers was striking. Hawkers, peddlers of diverse commodities, and laborers of all kinds and talents wandered the countryside and the towns. "In the seventeenth century the 'Cries of London' include thirty-seven different crafts and commodities."[28] This panoply of goods and services was to reach a crescendo of variety on the streets of nineteenth-century London. Many of these occupations were sorely disliked by the authorities. Singled out for special contempt were the tinkers, itinerant sellers and repairers of metal goods such as pots and pans; their bad reputation survives in current language with the verb "to tinker" and the expression "not worth a tinker's damn." The tinker, it seems, was not only obstreperous and disruptive, but was also prone to theft. At times, Beier notes, the tinkerer would coerce a potential client with an implicit threat: "let me mend your pots and pans—or else"! Further, the craft of tinkering was widely practiced by Gypsies, a people hated and feared not only because of their nomadic life but also because of their racial stigma.

Petty chapmen were also held in contempt. Though they peddled a variety of necessary items—pins, ribbons, tacks, combs, and other such articles—they were persecuted by the authorities as swindlers or, at least, pests. "Sales at this level were little more than bribes to be gone."[29] The forlorn apple peddler of depression-era America or the blind man silently hawking his pencils may be today's counterparts of the chapman of old.

Not all times were so chaotic and dismal. By the eighteenth century England had achieved a certain amount of political and economic stability. For reasons known only to demographers, the rapid and steady increase in population of the preceding two centuries had reached a plateau of some five millions (although it was to begin a phenomenal growth again within a few decades), consumer prices had stabilized, labor was in greater demand, and wages increased. The government's obsession with vagrancy declined. The Settlement Act of 1662 had, paradoxically, both legitimized vagrancy and established a policy of relief for the unfortunate transient. Another factor that served to attenuate the vagrancy problem was impressment, the forced enlistment of sailors or soldiers. Impressment increased substantially because England was at war for almost half the period between 1688 and 1756. During the reign of Queen Anne 200,000 men were under arms. The American colonies also provided a significant outlet for vagrants—some 150,000 persons had emigrated by the year 1700.[30] The number of jails, workhouses, and houses of correction increased considerably. The long years of legislative experimentation in respect to the vagrant had had an effect. He was, in that brief period, off the streets and not so disturbingly visible.

The last quarter of the eighteenth century brought the beginnings of industrialization and a revolution that would forever change the face of Western life. It may have been, as Steven Marcus claims, the only permanent revolution. It would grow in momentum through the nineteenth century and bring with it a new set of horrors for working men and women.[31] What had been basically a peasant society would be transformed within a very few decades into an industrial society; what had been a rural people was to become a city people. The industrial revolution gave rise to a variety of novel social problems: industrial poverty (which was not at all like the old and familiar poverty of agrarian England); urban congestion and squalor; deadly epidemics that can only arise in the midst of large, crowded populations living in unsanitary conditions; the disintegration and demoralization of family life; a kind of crime that is uniquely characteristic of large cities; and the unemployment that finally finds a name. To contemporary ears it might seem strange that the English word *unemployment* did not come into general use until the 1890s. But during the previous centuries the language could only offer the designation "idleness"—a word that carried with it, as we have seen, connotations of willfulness and individual deficit. Even Karl Marx, who clearly knew differently, was forced to use the expression *die Unbeschäftigen*, loosely translated as "the not busy."[32]

The industrial revolution also brought with it a new form of the old vagrancy problem: the urban vagrant.

Cotton ignited the process of industrialization in nineteenth-century England, the cotton that could be woven into cloth and shipped to markets all over the world. The cloth industry had been an important element in the English economy for several centuries, but with the advent of mechanical power and new technology, the industry burst into a frenzy of productivity. People swarmed into the midland cities from the bucolic hinterlands. Manchester's population growth was phenomenal: By the mid-1840s the Manchester-Salford area was an unbroken urban space of over 400,000 people.

Other industries and other cities experienced a similar explosion of growth. To say that a profound social chaos was engendered is to vastly understate what was really a catastrophe for the emerging working class. I do not have time or space here to discuss the vicissitudes of the Industrial Revolution, a tale that could fill libraries. It was both wonderful and horrible; a testimony to man's genius and to his selfishness; a time of opportunity for some and of calamity for others; of hope and of despair; of elegance and of filth. For wage laborers, the majority, it was a time of great hazard. They lacked trade unions and therefore a voice in the marketplace; they lacked the vote, and therefore a voice in government; and they lacked any kind of welfare system. The market was free and unfettered, wildly so, and subject to rapid and unpredictable oscillations of expansion and deflation that were beyond anybody's control or even understanding. The laborer under the best of conditions was often poor. A depression thus meant disaster.

English literature offers no better source about the evils of the Industrial Revolution and especially its human cost than the

Table 1–1
Estimated Population of Manchester
(1773–1851)

1773	24,000
1801	70,000
1831	142,000
1841	217,000
1851	250,000

works of Charles Dickens. His portraits are not romantic; they have all the force of Marx and Engels without the analysis and commentary. A small sample:

> Stokers emerged from low underground doorways into factory yards, and sat on steps, and posts, and palings, wiping their swarthy visages, and contemplating coals. The whole town seemed to be frying in oil. There was a stifling smell of hot oil elsewhere. The steam-engines shone with it, the dresses of the Hands were soiled with it, the mills throughout their many stories oozed and trickled it.[33]

The city described here was Manchester and Leeds and every other factory town; and if it sizzled in oil it was also suffocating in soot and filth and covered all over with the deadly pallor of human misery.

Working people were always on the edge of calamity. Sometimes they would fall into the sink of the underclass, emerge for a spell, and then descend once again. Like their counterparts during the age of the Stuarts, only now in much greater numbers, they were at risk of becoming the marginally employed, vagrants, or criminals. But their locus now was the great city rather than the town or village. The new cities were totally unplanned and housing for the working class and those further down the ladder was often wretched or worse.

> The catastrophe was worst in the great industrial towns where density and overcrowding went hand in hand with the interests of speculative builders, medieval administrative procedures and regulations—where they in fact existed—and produced a situation in which millions of grown people and their children were compelled to live in houses and neighborhoods that were without drains and often without sewers—and where sewers existed they took the runoff of street water and not waste from houses—without running water—sometimes not even in an entire neighborhood—and with one privy shared by who knows how many people: in some parts of Manchester over two hundred people shared a single privy. . . . Streets were often unpaved, and where they were paved no provision often existed for their cleansing. And large numbers of people lived in cellars, below the level of the street and below the water line.[34]

The distinction between living in a cellar cave and living in a doorway is one for pedants. Basically, the two domiciles were interchangeable for a great many of the cities' inhabitants. When a worker lost his job as a result of market forces, he lost the ability to pay rent for his barely habitable apartment, and he and his family were out on the streets. And these conditions, of course, were not restricted to Manchester, England's second city. Living in the workingman's quarters of all emerging cities was living in excrement. This is not a metaphor—it is a literal fact. And it was also true of America's cities: witness the influential, muckraking report of Jacob Riis.[35] And it is, alas, too true this very day in the monster cities of the developing world—Lagos, Cairo, São Paulo, Mexico City, Manila, and far too many others.[36] Homelessness, then, in newly industrialized cities, whether yesterday or today, is characterized by the same kinds of desperation.

The laboring men and women of London did not escape the disaster. In fact, they became the focus of a newly developing philanthropic concern—a care that eventually evolved into the elaborate apparatus of good intention and public policy called the Welfare State. The "street people" of London were a bustling and variegated lot, all too visible to the more fortunate classes of that great city. The classic study of the English underclass written by Henry Mayhew is a marvel of detail wherein he treats all manner of sights, sounds, smells, and people—in four packed volumes. His *London Labour and the London Poor* (1861–62) is stunning testimony to what a dedicated observer can accomplish. London was amok with rat killers, acrobats, conjurers, clowns, stiltmen, "Ethiopian" serenaders, garrote masters, coal whippers, ballast heavers, lumpers, lightermen, ticket porters, destroyers of vermin, mudlarks, prostitutes, and many, many others—all living on the thin edge of life itself and all, at one moment or another, vagrant.

Mayhew, like many others, was not oblivious to what was so blatantly obvious: many decent and hard-working people fell into hard times and were wasted by their impoverishment. But he was faced with the eternal question of how to distinguish between the true victim and the scoundrel:

The evils consequent upon the uncertainty of labour I have already been at considerable pains to point out. There is still

one other mischief attendant upon it that remains to be exposed, and which, if possible, is greater than any other yet
adduced . . . a large class of wayfarers . . . those vagabond
or erratic spirits who find continuity of application to any task
specially irksome to them, and who are physically or mentally
unwilling to remain for any length of time in the same place,
or at the same work—creatures who are vagrants in disposition
and principle; the wandering tribe of this country; the nomads
of the present day.[37]

But he cannot tell the difference between the vagrant and his
more honorably worthy! They look the same, they act the same—
and though he himself did not recognize the fact—perhaps they
were the same. The vagrant of nineteenth-century London was
physically real but he, and certainly she, remained a conceptual
phantom.

He or she was a person—as were most of those in the underclass—of many vices and debilities. The vagrant was sickly
and suffered from the ravages of tuberculosis, typhus, cholera,
scrofula, rickets, or various other disorders too numerous to
mention. He or she was apt to be a member of the despised races
from the Celtic fringe—Wales, Ireland, and Scotland. He or she
often turned to ale and stronger spirits to escape misery.

Further, like his or her worker brethren, the vagrant had a
predilection for opiates and other narcotic nostrums, including
a seemingly popular tonic called Godfrey's Cordial.[38] Thomas
De Quincey had occasion to observe that "some years ago, on
passing through Manchester, I was informed by several cotton
manufacturers that their work people were rapidly getting into
the practice of opium-eating, so much so that on a Saturday
afternoon the counter of the druggists were strewed with pills
of one, two, or three grains, in preparation for the known demand of the evening."[39] This widespread use of opiates was repeatedly confirmed by other observers.

The vagrant life was characterized by all the usual depravi-
ties: sexual license, bastardy, prostitution, theft, swindling, etc.
The inventory of vice and disrepute is by now familiar. Indeed,
it is much like the litany intoned by moralists in respect to the
homeless of our own time.

The good people of England were not troubled by this large
swarm of marginal labor because they offended the nostrils or

because they were an affront to decency and morality. The good people were troubled because they feared the underclass as a *political* threat. They were, indeed, the "dangerous classes." A roll of frightening events instigated by the marginal people of England would include "the Gordon riots of 1780, the mobbing of the king in 1795, the Spa Field riot in 1816, the Queen Caroline riots of 1820, the Reform riots of 1832, . . . the Sunday trading riots of 1855, the anti-Tractarian riots."[40] This list omits the Luddites of 1811, who rose up to sabotage the hated machines, and the Chartists, who agitated for a variety of reforms, both political and economic. And, of course, there were Engels and Marx with their manifesto of 1848 and the continental revolutions of that momentous year.

There was, in short, the mob—a specter of revolutionary France and hated Jacobins to bother the sleep of English squires and solid merchants. But the English mob did not materialize like its counterpart in Paris. The "residuum" behaved itself—more or less.

We find then, as the twentieth century approached, not so much a cauldron as a chemist's graduated cylinder filled with a viscous labor force, the higher levels rather stable and forming a middle class of workers, the lower levels blending into more tenuous strata of unskilled wage earners, casuals, vagrants, and lumpen proletariat.[41] These lower levels, by no means numerically small, were extremely fluid, with people drifting up and down in the cylinder of marginal labor and faced still on a daily basis with the prospect of economic and social disaster. It is a condition confronted to this day by the underclass.

But enough of England. Vagrancy in that country continued throughout the rest of the nineteenth century and still exists today. It has had its ups and downs, as we would by now expect, sometimes attracting more and sometimes less public attention. It surely has dropped significantly since the rise of the trade unions and the growth of the British welfare state with its unemployment insurance and other public aid devices for people in need. Yet vagrancy continues to trouble the perceptions and sometimes the conscience of Britain.[42] But what of the New World with its glorious possibility and its fresh start?

2

The American Contribution:

Mountain Men, Forty-niners, Cowboys, Hoboes, and Bums

L IFE, in early colonial America, was hard for everybody. Subsistence was scratched from a stubborn, stony soil; few amenities were available—even if one had the money to purchase them; and native Indians did not always take kindly to interlopers. Colonial life by definition was one of poverty. The frontier was everywhere. But land was everywhere, too, just for the taking. Thus there was no reason for anyone to be a landless peasant or a sturdy beggar.

The ships from England, as we have seen, brought not only vagrants but widows, orphans, bona fide criminals, lunatics, and misfits of all sorts from the motherland. What had been England's bane became this country's early treasure. How strange it is to think that the scoundrel, rogue, conniver, or criminal—the social misfit or moral defective—could become, as a result of a rigorous trip on the sailing vessels of the Atlantic and new opportunities in the New World, an industrious farmer or diligent apprentice! What transformations occurred when English failures became American successes!

The colonies had poverty but no idleness to speak of. At least for a while. Whatever need occurred was met by the community at large. Widows, orphans, and other such worthy poor folk would be rotated among the families of a community for several weeks at a time until they somehow found the wherewithal to support themselves.[1] Eventually, of course, as the colonies and their populations grew, this system of mutual support suffered strain and eventual collapse. Victims of fate, failures, and outcasts of one colony or community moved by their own choice or were expelled to other colonies or communities. As early as 1675, refugees from the uprising of Indians in Rhode Island known as King Philip's War arrived in Boston. Sixty-two people became public charges and had to be "warned away" and removed. Newport suffered a similar influx; the hapless refugees who fled to that city were likewise received with annoyance and even rancor.

The refugees presented a thorny problem for the new colonists: these people had lost their homes and sources of livelihood. They had become the "unsettled poor." The New World authorities began to treat their new society's economic failures and misfits according to the methods of Old World authorities. In 1631, for example, "One Abigail Gifford, widow, being kept at the charge of the parish Weldsen in Middlesex near London, was sent by Mr. Ball's ship to this country, and found to be somewhat distracted and a very burdensome woman, the governor and assistants returned her back by warrant . . . to the same parish in the ship *Rebecca.*"[2] Poor Abigail was probably one of the demented who earlier had been siphoned from the asylums and streets of England.

Many colonial failures solved their own problems by moving from north to south, south to north, or—most frequently—west. And if the settled communities turned against a misfit, he too had the option of escaping to the boundless frontier. In the early days this frontier was often just a few miles away; later it was located in Vermont, Maine, the Appalachians, the Carolinas, or Georgia. Movement became imbedded in the very spirit and soul of America. In the beginning everybody was a frontiersman or a pioneer; later, this way of life became an option—for the ambitious, for the adventurer, and also for the failure and the misfit.

The Cumberland was breached and the western frontier moved from Massachusetts to Kentucky and then on to Ohio and Illinois. What manner of people were these who undertook such epic journeys in order to face a life of hardship, deprivation, and danger? Most were farming families who wanted to do better. The frontier farm families, however, were preceded by others who had marked the way. These souls, the pathfinders of America, became the stuff of legend, the national heroes celebrated for their courage and fortitude. Many of them, perhaps most, were oddballs by any reckoning. In the Old World many would have been counted among the vagrant.

The archetype of such a person was the mountain man, a colossal figure out of which myth was made. He left the settlements and, during the first three decades of the nineteenth century, went west—to the real west, beyond the Mississippi and across the Missouri into the Rockies and beyond to hunt the beaver for its pelt. Alone, often *absolutely* alone, he traveled where no white man had ever been before: without maps, without landmarks, without any comprehension of what lay ahead. And he stayed in the wilderness with his traps and his growing load of pelts for months or years before rendezvousing with the buyers from the fur companies.

The life was mean, bitter, and solitary, but surely the mountain man must have craved his isolation. He lived alone by choice. But sometimes he "went native" and took up with the Indians: Blackfoot, Crow, Nez Perce. He might take a "wife" and father children, he might dress in Indian clothes, and he might participate in their hunts and raiding parties. A few became indistinguishable from the braves of the tribes that had adopted them; some even achieved honor and distinction among the Indian nations.[3]

Sometimes the Indians would kill a mountain man or make him their captive. Fierce animals, especially the grizzly bear, endangered his existence. The great character, part true to life and part fiction, Liver Eatin' Johnson, was severely mauled by a grizzly bear and left to die by his impatient companion. Johnson, half-dead and horribly mutilated, crawled for *hundreds* of miles back to what might have passed for civilization—driven by his dreams of taking vengeance against the man who had abandoned him. Sure enough, Johnson eventually found the traitor and, according to legend, in his frenzy he tore the poor man's liver from the still-warm corpse and devoured it. Hence, the nickname Liver

Eatin' Johnson—a mountain man in the grand tradition. Did it happen like this? No matter, Johnson like his peers became a legend that typified the loner who goes west to make his way and forge a nation.

The very geography sings of the stuff out of which romance is built. There are the great rivers: the Missouri, the Platte, the Bitterroot, the Yellowstone, the Snake, the Bighorn; the Indian tribes: Mandan, Oglala, Crow, Nez Perce, Blackfoot, Flathead; the mountains: the Grand Teton, Uinta, and the Wind River; the places: Jackson Hole, Henry's Fork, Cache Valley. Even today, in a world of asphalt and stainless steel, these place-names have the ability to raise the spirit. Coupled with the rugged individuals who wandered these virgin terrains, heroic legend becomes irresistible.

But the mountain man was a tool—an essential instrument for the rapacious fur companies. The pelt of the industrious beaver was a valuable commodity used primarily for felting until the industrialized cloth industry was able to fabricate much cheaper felt materials. But it was also used for hats and by the 1840s for coats. The English Hudson's Bay Company was first to exploit the beaver. Its free-lance trappers hunted all over Canada. A chartered monopoly, it merged with its greatest rival, the Northwest Company, and established its central operational headquarters at Fort Vancouver, British Columbia.

The Americans were not far behind the English. John Jacob Astor organized the American Fur Company. During the prime years of the beaver trade his company was locked in a ferocious competition with the Rocky Mountain Fur Company. The great companies also had smaller, "independent" competitors. De Bonneville and Wyeth from Cambridge, Massachusetts, were among the more important of these smaller entrepreneurs. Many of the personalities who were agents or employees of the fur companies went on to become well known: Kenneth McKenzie, Jim Bridger, Kit Carson, and Milton Sublette are among those whose names can be recognized even today.

The mountain man worked for these companies—sometimes as a free agent selling his pelts to the highest bidder, more often as a contract trapper who received a stipend as well as a commission on the number of pelts he collected. When the struggle between the companies became intense, the mountain man did well. The Rocky Mountain Fur Company, for example, had to pay as high as $1500 to expert trappers to keep them out of the hands of Astor's trust. This payment was a bonus; the trapper could receive an additional nine dollars a pound for the beaver pelts themselves.[4] But when the competition eased off, the bonus might disappear altogether and the dollar value for pelts declined accordingly. The more typical going rate for beaver was four dollars a pound.

But what the fur companies gave with one hand they took away with the other. The fur companies, at their annual rendezvous, charged trappers such outrageous prices as ten dollars a yard for cloth that sold for fourteen cents a yard in St. Louis and two dollars a pound for flour that could be had for two cents in the same gateway city. And they made equally obscene profits on whiskey (five dollars a pint and diluted to boot), tobacco, gunpowder, lead, traps, horses, and many other necessities for the work of trapping and trading with the Indians.[5] By the time the mountain man sobered up and finished with the rendezvous to start another year of solitude he was often impoverished again. The fur companies had their pelts for the price of some bad whiskey and a few trifles that had been brought up, admittedly with considerable hardship, from St. Louis. There, each spring would be found a few score of new young men making ready to set out for the trip up the Missouri and the Platte into the pristine wilderness.

His epic heroism notwithstanding, the mountain man was a sucker. In the end, most had nothing material to show for their years of hardship. Otherwise, they were left with incredible tales to tell in their dotage and the posthumous satisfaction that comes with being a legend. John Astor did considerably better.

The reign of the mountain man was short-lived, perhaps two decades, for by the 1840s the beaver trade had all but disappeared. But a new promise emerged to attract the solitary when gold was discovered in the foothills of the Sierra Nevada. James Marshall, in the process of setting up a sawmill for John Sutter on the south fork of the American River, stumbled upon a few bits of the glittering yellow metal in January 1848. The news spread with amazing rapidity in spite of the vast distance between

California and the eastern settlements. And once again, as in times long past, disaffected and rootless young men set out on long journeys of hope and promise, this time to gather nuggets of gold. The attraction of easy pickings drew these young people not only from the East but from all over the world; Europe, South America, and even Asia sent men to the great gold rush. The trip from the eastern seaboard may have been by ship down the South Atlantic, around Cape Horn, and then up the eastern edge of the Pacific to wild San Francisco. Treacherous Cape Horn could be bypassed by disembarking in Panama, trekking across the isthmus, and taking another ship to complete the Pacific leg of the journey. Some traveled totally overland, but that was a more difficult and time-consuming route. Since the land route could take a whole spring and summer, it was mainly a path for those who could not muster the fare for the expensive journey by sea.

San Francisco, once a sleepy nothing, was now a booming chaos. Sailors and masters abandoned their ships in the bay and hurried to the hills. The harbor became a forest of forsaken vessels left to rot. The town itself was intoxicated with gold and the promise of wealth. Gamblers, prostitutes, saloon keepers, and sharpies of all kinds descended upon the shacks and shanties that comprised the emerging city. Tradesmen and merchants moved in to tend to the needs of the impatient prospectors, itching to get to the hills before all the nuggets were picked clean. Most, of course, couldn't tell a gold nugget from a chip of granite, nor did they realize that extracting gold from its hiding places usually required hard and sophisticated labor. Some learned.

Costs beggared the imagination. In San Francisco during the first couple of years after the strike, apples sold for one to five dollars each, eggs sold for ten to fifty dollars a dozen, butcher knives cost thirty dollars, a blanket forty dollars, and boots of good quality cost a hundred dollars a pair. Common iron tacks were literally worth their weight in gold; a *pound* of gold bought a *pound* of tacks. In the camps, of course, prices were considerably higher. And, of course, miners were the prey of all kinds of sharks: gamblers, saloon keepers, dancing girls, lawyers, and claim jumpers.[6]

The saloons, at first nothing more than canvas tents and shacks, did a thriving business. In the city and in the camps they were invariably coupled with gambling tables. The prospector, even if he were fortunate enough to strike it rich, had little chance to escape the cupidity of a long line of sharpies out to make their own strike. Alcohol was the undoing of many a miner. Narcotics were ubiquitous; substances such as opium had already become a part of disaffiliated life. By the late 1870s San Francisco had large numbers of drug addicts who lived in the alleys of Chinatown and the Barbary Coast. "They eked out a bare existence by panhandling, by running errands for the brothel-keepers and inmates, and by collecting wood and old boxes, which they sold to Chinese merchants and householders."[7]

The influx of people was huge and rapid, as Rodman Paul indicates: "Both the federal census of 1850 and the state census of 1852 were incomplete and inaccurate. Stated tersely, there seem to have been about 14,000 persons, other than Indians, in California when the rush began in 1848; by the close of 1849 several less than 100,000; by the latter part of 1852, perhaps 250,000; by 1860, 380,000."[8] Not all were in the mines by any means; Paul estimates that in 1852 some 100,000 men were actually working at the diggings, but their numbers then began to shrink as the pickings became more stubborn and the extraction of gold became more technologically complex.

The early censuses revealed that over 90 percent of the California population was male; in the gold regions that proportion was even larger. Most women remained in the seaboard communities; those that went to the camps were saloon girls and whores.

The miners were young. Many moved from dig to dig and camp to camp in a perpetual search for pay dirt. The majority were American—two-thirds according to the 1850 census. Other miners came from Europe and South America; there were large numbers of Chinese and also a much smaller number of Malays.[9] The Americans were mostly from the "west," states such as Ohio and Missouri; a surprising number of miners were New Englanders, but relatively few were southerners. They were city boys and farm boys and some who had no past that they wanted to speak of:

Oh, what was your name in the States?
Was it Thompson or Johnson or Bates?

Did you murder your wife
And flee for your life?
Say, what was your name in the States?[10]

In a very short time the easily obtained gold, that found by placer mining, had been picked clean. Finding the rest required the technically complex and expensive process of hydraulic mining or the even more difficult task of deep mining. Both these methods required large amounts of capital, technical skills and equipment, and managerial expertise far beyond the capacities of most miners. Thus many forty-niners settled down to family life and the more prosaic employments of farming, ranching, mercantile trade, and wage labor. Others, however, became itinerant miners ready to hurry off at the first word of a new gold strike, wherever it might be. Inspired by rumor and misinformation, these frantic journeys might take him to such disappointing places as Kern River, which generated a hysteria in 1855; or to the Fraser River in British Columbia where there were reports of fabulous wealth in 1858.[11] Both of these reports turned out to be false, but many others all over the West and in Canada and Alaska would prove to be true, providing new stimulus for gold fever for decades.

In brief, what remained of the forty-niner was a mining proletariat: a small army of technically adept, skilled, and knowledgeable workers who became a critical component of this country's mining industry. They were the new pathfinders of the West, this time moving—paradoxically—from the settlements on the Pacific coast to the still unpopulated east of the Cordilleran plateau. These miners, once teenagers and now becoming grizzled with age and the weather, searched in succession for gold, silver, and then the less exotic metals such as lead and copper. Their hallmark was a mobility that verged on nomadism; they had no permanent residence, and were unattached to kin or community. They embodied, to an extreme perhaps, the country's ethos: pick up and move. They suffered from illness; they were lonely; they had many of the marks that had been ascribed to their counterparts of earlier generations: the tendency to abuse chemical substances, a bit of roguery, and a touch of mental illness. They were the harbingers of what was soon to follow to swell the ranks of solitary and unattached migratory labor: the American hobo.

The end of the Civil War marked the beginning of an explosive settlement of the West. Disbanded armies always leave in their wake substantial numbers of young men who cannot go home and will not settle down. In the South, especially, the established way of life had been disrupted or totally destroyed in many areas. Demoralized veterans returned home, were dissatisfied with what they found or didn't find, and drifted away. The enticements of the West offered glorious possibilities. Land was cheap, indeed free if one were willing to work it. And there were the railroads, pushing forward into the prairies and even through the rugged mountains, to link the country and the new lands to the Eastern heartland.

The rails had to be laid. The East Coast was already latticed with a fabric of wood ties and steel rails that did much to promote the growing industries and commerce of the area. By 1860 Milwaukee, St. Louis, Memphis, New Orleans, and Chicago were part of the network of track. And by 1866 the Union Pacific and the Central Pacific were under construction.[12] The two lines met in desolate Utah in 1869 and the continent was finally joined by an unbroken band of steel rails. Between 1867 and 1873 some 30,000 miles of new track were laid; by 1893, 150,000 miles of track crisscrossed the country—a stupendous feat of construction.[13] The spread of the railroad to the West generated enormous fortunes for the Huntingtons, Stanfords, Hills, and Cookes; more, perhaps, derived from the land that came with the right-of-way—generously given by a rather corrupt Congress—than from freight tariffs. These people were to become the folk heroes of American industry and capitalism. But there were other folk heroes, too, the men who laid the track: the gandy dancers and spike men.

Many railroad workers were Irish immigrants. Fleeing the Great Famine and its aftermath, millions of Irish immigrated to America. But many received a cold welcome: their brogue and their Catholicism marked them as "different" and suspect. Chinese miners, after gleaning what they could from the leavings of departed placer prospectors, were hired by the Southern Pacific—along with newly recruited coolies from the continent of Asia—to do the very dangerous work of blasting and tunneling through the Sierras. They, too, were not made welcome by a frightened and chauvinistic working class. And, of course, there were home-grown misfits to supplement the gangs of Irish and Chinese who, together, bound the nation tightly with rails of steel. The track had to be laid, but first the bed had to be graded—no mean task in the steep mountains. And after the track was down, wood was required to feed the engines' fireboxes and water to boil the steam. And tracks needed to be walked and cared for, trestles repaired, and wire strung to carry the telegraphy. The railroads were an *industry,* and it required large numbers of casual, unskilled workers. The residuum of America and Europe was there to fill the need.

The West also provided a home for the cowboy, stalwart of a cattle industry that would eventually feed not only the expanding population of America but the populace of Europe as well. Beef cattle had been raised for meat since the earliest colonial days but, except for the large ranches of Mexico, ranching had always been conducted on a very small scale. The real heyday of American ranching began in Texas immediately after the Civil War. Texas, though a Confederate state, had been spared the ravages of the war. Local herds had grown large and fat during the war; there had been few hands to tend to the herds and fewer markets where they could be sold at a profit. That all changed in the spring of 1866 when the first Texas herds were driven north to Abilene, Kansas, where a railhead had been established to meet them. The journey was hard; nobody seemed to know the way or, at least, the best route. The cattle were not always cooperative and stampeded easily. Cowboys had not yet gained needed experience in managing herds of the size that were negotiating the trail. Indians were a problem—not because they killed cowboys or cattle, but because they often charged exorbitant fees for the use of the grass and the water. Resident Kansans were even more difficult; some local herds had been decimated by a cattle disease, Texas fever, that had been blamed on infected Texas herds. Luckless cowpokes were often met by armed locals blocking their transit.

The rewards to the rancher barons were enormous. In 1867 a three-year-old steer could be bought in Texas for nine dollars; the same animal brought eighty-six dollars in Massachusetts and seventy dollars in New Jersey.[14] In the first postwar drive of 1866 some 260,000 head of longhorns began the journey. Probably fewer than half survived but much was learned, and the later drives were more successful. Very shortly, cattle country extended north through Nebraska, Colorado, Wyoming, and into Montana. Abilene lost its primacy as a railhead, much to the relief of new farming settlers who yearned for a more tranquil township. The infamous Dodge City next became the destination of choice for the cattle drivers.

Within a few years the profitability of ranching attracted the attention of Eastern and continental capital. Some of the large ranches were bought up by these investors. In 1870 W. J. Menzies founded the Scottish American Investment Company, which ultimately controlled several cattle companies in the Great Plains and Wyoming. English, Scottish, and even French investors gained control over ranches that were the size of some European principalities. Some of these foreigners came to this country to personally oversee operations, much to the chagrin of the native cowboy who had once enjoyed a close and working camaraderie with his boss.[15]

Like much else in booming America, ranching became a large and complex industry. Prior to the huge influx of capital, the great ranch—under the control of its hardworking owner—had much in common with the feudal estate of medieval Europe. A medieval lord would not have felt much out of place running a large ranch, with its ranch house, outlying sheds, bunkhouses, barns, and storerooms; its immense lands; and the men on horseback waiting to do his bidding. He would have enjoyed the entertainments, much like jousts of old, in which the cowhands would demonstrate their skill and prowess at riding and roping; occasional forays against Indians and intruding neighbors; and even a unique coat of arms, his brand emblazoned on the flanks of all his cattle. It is no coincidence that owners of great ranches were called cattle barons. Within their own domain the ranchers imposed their own laws and meted out their own justice.

The cowboy was usually young, often a teenager. His very name testifies to his age; unless he owned the ranch, he was never referred to as a "cowman." "You never saw an old cowpuncher. They were scarce as hen's teeth. Where they went to, heaven only knows."[16] They probably went where the mountain men and the miners before them went, back home to the farm or the city to grub out the remainder of their lives in a more sedentary labor. Most men quit the work after ten or fifteen years. Injuries were common and the "stove-up" cowboy might spend the rest of his life nursing his health.[17] He came, originally, from Texas. But as the word spread about plenty of jobs in a big country, young lads from all over made the trek to the plains. The life was hard: wake early to round up strays, ride fence, break horses, minister to sick calves, and see that the water flowed smoothly from windmills. On the great drives, the newcomer would ride in the rear to spur on the laggard beasts—and after fourteen hours in the saddle he would have inhaled pounds of dust and dirt. The more experienced cowboys would guard the flanks of the great herds or ride point, behind the trail boss who paved the way. To the rear of the trail boss was the chuck wagon under the domain of the high-ranking and well-paid cook. A good cook could make as much money as a trail boss and was in great demand.

Cowboys often moved from ranch to ranch—always with the belief that things would be better elsewhere. The hands did not stay long: "The records of the Spur Ranch in west Texas show that some young men began working on April first and quit on the seventh, twelfth, or the fourteenth of the same month. A few left because they were homesick, others because the hard work was not as interesting or as romantic as the eastern literature of the day had suggested."[18] On the SMS ranch, in a period beginning in 1885, only 3 percent of the hands worked as many as five consecutive seasons; 64 percent remained for only one season.[19] And the work *was* seasonal: the northern ranches required few hands in the winter. Montana, Colorado, and Wyoming cowboys might then wander south to see what they could pick up on the Texas spreads where the search for water required many range riders. Many out-of-work cowboys holed up in towns to drink away the winter. The wandering cowboy was a reality:

> *I am a wandering cowboy,*
> *From ranch to ranch I roam;*
> *At every ranch when welcome,*
> *I make myself at home.*

Two years I worked for the Double L,
And one for the O Bar O;
Then drifted west from Texas,
To the plains of Mexico . . .

It is now I'm tired of rambling.
No longer will I roam
When my pony I've unsaddled
In the old corral at home.[20]

Alas, the retiring cowboy might not even own his own horse. This essential animal was usually furnished by the owner from among a herd of horses, trained for different tasks, and provided by the rancher for the hands he hired. The retired cowboy was fortunate if he had amassed even a few hundred dollars to start him on a new life. Wages were modest: in 1872, a new hand might get $20 a month "work or play," but there was little time for play. By 1885, a typical wage was $38; that dropped to $32 in 1890. Top hands could get as much as $45. But a good cook was worth $65 a month.[21]

The inevitable whiskey, card sharks, and wild, wild women waited in such towns as Abilene, Wichita, and Dodge City when the poor cowboy came in from the drive. His wages couldn't last long among that mass of hungry fellows. The cowboy sometimes joined the predators: out-of-work, he "usually degenerated, drifted, disappeared, or worse still, became a saloonkeeper."[22] Sometimes he went East, or up to Chicago, to lose himself among the throngs of hoboes. At other times he became an outlaw; Billy the Kid is the prototype of the child-cowboy turned bad.

The free range was eventually fenced in with the aid of newly invented barbed wire. With the end of the open range, farms grew up and farmers replaced cowboys throughout much of the West. Even where ranches and cowboys survived, "Old Paint" was eventually replaced by the pick-up truck. Few cowboys are left today.

Migratory labor opened the West. Mountain men, miners, railroad workers, and cowboys paved the way for settlement and agriculture. But migratory and casual labor also *sustained* the West—and the rest of the country. There was plenty of back-breaking work to be done. Much of it was seasonal or subject to the benignity of the weather. All of it was poorly paid. The

American labor force began to differentiate into two groups: a skilled, settled industrial proletariat beginning to achieve some stability, security, and protection from economic oscillation, and a marginal labor force—a "reserve," a *residuum* of the untrained, unskilled, and unsettled, many of whom lived on the edge of convention and law. Throughout the remainder of this book, I will have many occasions to refer again to this residuum.

The migratory worker, whom I will hereafter usually call a hobo, by the last decade of the nineteenth century still had plenty to occupy himself. Ranch hands were still needed. Mining was an option. Rails were still being laid, even if the halcyon days were over. The lumber industry of the Northwest, ice harvesting in the northern states in the winter months, the building and construction trades, and—the great sponge for casual labor—farming offered opportunities for seasonal work. Agriculture had always been labor-hungry, especially at harvest time when the crops must be picked within the very narrow window of a few weeks or even a few days. The American farm always had the greatest demand for marginal labor, dwarfing the demand required by mines, ranches, and logging operations combined. And that need remained through the turn of the century and, though much diminished, survives to this very day.

The hobo worked at these various jobs, trudging from place to place by foot and, when the distances were large, riding the very rails that he might have helped to lay. Riding the rails was a dangerous way to travel. Trying to jump a moving freight train could easily end in miscalculation and death: 2,553 people met this sad fate in 1919; another 2,166 died the following year.[23] These figures include trespassers of all kinds; the railroads did not, and perhaps could not, distinguish between hoboes and others who might have been killed on their trains or properties. Mutilations and injuries, too, took a toll: for the same years, injuries totaled 2,658 and 2,362 respectively. Obviously, death was as likely as injury; several tons of boxcar could as easily kill as maim. The hobo always preferred to ride a boxcar—if he could get inside. Often he rode the wooden catwalk above, and sometimes he rode in the tender. The worst and most perilous place was under the very carriage of the cars, inches above the wheels; this was called "riding the rods." Some brakemen and conductors enjoyed making the hoboes' access to the boxcars as difficult and dangerous as possible.

Being killed or injured was not the most common risk attendant on or associated with hopping a freight. Private policemen, Pinkerton men—the railroad "bulls"—often beat and clubbed hoboes. The railroads hated hoboes, not only because they affronted management by getting, free, a ride that more decent people had to pay for, but because hoboes also stole from the trains. Not very much, but in the process of rummaging and rifling among the variety of goods carried by the freights, the hobo made at least a tiny dent in profits. T. T. Kelihor, chief special agent of the Illinois Central Railroad, complained that:

> The average hobo realizes that he is not provided with means of carrying away a large amount of bulky goods. Consequently when hobos enter a merchandise car, they break open a great many cases and dump or throw out the contents on the floor in searching for small, compact, valuable goods that they then can carry off concealed about their persons.[24]

Kelihor goes on to estimate that the railroad's loss in damaged goods is more than ten times its loss for hobo thefts. I should note here that many hoboes considered these allegations of theft to be much exaggerated. The real problem, they claimed, was pilfering by railroad employees who blamed hoboes to cover their own thefts. But we should not be too quick to absolve the hobo; homeless people do not have the same attachment, let alone affection, for the sanctity of private property. As a marginal man, the hobo did not hold many values common to more established members of society.

In any event, war was constant between the men who rode the rods and those charged with protecting railroad property. It was an even struggle: the private police had the advantage of resources and legal sanction; the hoboes had an informal network of information and intelligence. Hoboes knew which yards to avoid, which schedules were more benign, which towns to bypass altogether, and which "bulls" were more ferocious. Some private policemen gained notorious reputations among the hoboes and word would rapidly spread about their rousting tactics.

Green River, Wyoming, was proud of a bull known to the hobo confederation as "Green River Slim," a man to be avoided at all costs. Word of Slim's habits spread quickly, and remedial strategies were devised accordingly.[25]

The public police forces were unwilling partners of the private police in this chronic battle. Their fundamental interest was in keeping the hobo out of town, so they did not take kindly to the railroad's habit of dumping unsavories into the local jail. The railroads wanted the hapless hobo off their trains, the locals wanted them anywhere else but in their town, and the hobo wanted only to get to where he was going in the hope of picking up a few dollars.

The jungle became his habitat. Usually located near a railroad junction, but also sometimes close by highways, the hobo jungle provided shelter for a day or two—occasionally more—for the traveling hobo. The jungle community provided companionship, intelligence as to the temper of police, where jobs might be found, and news in general, and solace from the pain of living. A typical hobo jungle would be close to a water supply, within walking distance of a general store, and in a dry and shady place. Ideally, it would be located near a town but not so close as to provoke the displeasure of the townspeople. Errors in siting judgment were made, however; the good village folk sometimes turned from tolerance to nontolerance, and then might gather in the dark of night with torches, clubs, and shotguns to drive the hoboes away and burn down their shelters. As we have seen, communities—at least since Elizabethan times—often address their "homeless problem" by driving the homeless away.

Hobo ballads capture the feel of the life. Here, in an excerpt from "The Gila Monster Route" by a nameless wanderer, the perils of the life become clear:

> *The lingering sunset across the plain*
> *Kissed the rear end of an east-bound train,*
> *And shone on the passing track close by*
> *Where a dingbat sat on a rotten tie . . .*
>
> *There was nothing in sight but sand and space;*
> *No chance for a bo to feed his face;*

Not even a shack to beg for a lump.
Nor a hen house there to frisk for a gump . . .

Then, down by the tracks, in the jungle's glade,
On the cool, green grass in the tule's shade,
They shed their coats, and ditched their shoes,
And tanked up full of that colored booze.

Then, they took a flop with their hides plumb full,
And did not hear the harness bull,
Till he shook them out of their boozy nap,
With a husky voice and a loaded sap.[26]

The two pals celebrated in this ballad ended up in the local jail after a few good clouts on the head. One of the men, it is sung, had the misjudgment to later climb aboard a cattle car, where he was trampled to death.

The jungle was the great socializing institution of American tramp life. Fledglings learned the rules and the codes of behavior, the most precious of which was everyone's right to privacy and anonymity. Most other proscriptions revolved around the safety and well-being of the jungle community: no fires at night, no joining in the communal meal without scavenging wood before eating and helping to clean up after eating, and otherwise conforming to the few simple injunctions that made for a tolerable habitat. "Mulligan's stew" was the communal meal, a concoction of *anything* edible tossed into a kettle to blend with other mysterious or nameless ingredients. Stories were told, songs were sung, old newspapers were passed around, and legends grew out of elaboration and fabrication.

The jungle was not completely secure even within itself. Theft was widespread—hobo jungle codes of behavior notwithstanding. Violence sometimes occurred. The drinking of spirits often led to unpredictability of behavior. Children and teenagers were often the targets of older "buzzards." Sexual abuse of young boys was a hazard they all had to face; many did not escape the coercion of the "wolves" who stalked them. Hobo life was a life without women: in all such societies homosexuality is rampant.

In the first decade of the twentieth century, hoboes sometimes needed proof of proper political beliefs. Without a "red card," to demonstrate membership in the I.W.W.—the Wobblies—the politically indifferent hobo might be run out of the jungle by his more militant colleagues. Or he might be thrown off the train; having escaped the watchful eye of the "bull," a hobo could face the wrath of boxcar companions if he failed, then and there, to swear allegiance to the Wobblies.

The Industrial Workers of the World was theoretically a radical organization of all laborers who suffered under the yoke of wages. But its greatest appeal was among migratory workers. The hobo became identified in the public mind (and, of course, in the minds of police) with the I.W.W. Founded in 1905 in Chicago, the organization eventually claimed some 100,000 members, most of whom were, at any one time, on the road. Dues were fifty cents a month; most members were in arrears and not in good standing. For people vulnerable to the caprices of casual wage labor, the I.W.W. had great appeal. Its charter called for the *abolition* of wages altogether:

> The working class and the employing class have nothing in common. There can be no peace so long as hunger and want are found among millions of the working people and the few, who make up the employing class, have all the good things of life. . . .
>
> Instead of the conservative motto, "A fair day's wage for a fair day's work," we must inscribe on our banner the revolutionary watchword, "Abolition of the wage system."[27]

The turn-of-the-century hobo was in many surprising respects a political creature. He knew he was sorely used by an ungrateful economy and, perhaps caught up in contemporary Populism, he was ready to lend his support to movements that promised a fairer life. In 1894, in the midst of the economic panic that had begun the preceding year, the miserable unemployed gathered at Massillon, Ohio, under the banner of the "Commonweal of Christ." They were led by Jacob S. Coxey, a contractor, to begin a march to Washington so as to petition the president and the Congress for a program of public works.[28] "Coxey's Army" was joined by migratory workers at almost every railway junction—many coming from as far as California, whose battalions were led by such as "General" Charles T. Kelly and

"General" Lewis C. Fry. The army was met with little sympathy by townspeople and the press:

> *Hark, hark! Hear the dogs bark!*
> *Coxey is coming to town*
> *In his ranks are scamps*
> *And growler-fed tramps*
> *On all of whom workingmen frown.*[29]

The march produced no positive results. All it really established was a new American term for a congregation of the ragged, noisy, and disreputable: a "Coxey's Army."

Even the small farmer, caught up in the Populist cause that had been exemplified by Coxey's march, and so desperately dependent on the migratory worker at harvest time, did not take kindly to the hobo. The feeling was reciprocated:

> *We are coming home, John Farmer; We are coming back to stay.*
> *For nigh on fifty years or more, we've gathered up your hay.*
> *We have slept out in your hayfields; we have heard your morning*
> *   shout;*
> *We've heard you wondering where in hell's them pesky go-abouts?*
>
> *It's a long way, now understand me; it's a long way to town;*
> *It's a long way across the prairies, and to hell with Farmer Brown.*
> *Here goes for better wages, and the hours must come down.*
> *For we're out for a winter's stake this summer, and we want no*
> *   scabs around.*
>
> *You've paid the going wages, that's what kept us on the bum*
> *You say you've done your duty, you chin-whiskered son-of-a-gun.*
> *We have sent your kids to college, but still you rave and shout*
> *And call us tramps and hobos, and pesky go-abouts.*[30]

Songs like this became part and parcel of the culture of hoboes. They reflect quite accurately what was a rather unique feature of these men—a feature absent in most earlier cohorts of vagrant people—a political consciousness, a very real sense that they were disembodied entries in the ledger of the American economy.

When the off-season was long and when the need for his services diminished, the hobo often sought shelter in the cities.

There he could winter among the cheap lodging houses, restaurants, missions, and bars of the area delimited for his use by a watchful police. There he would blend into the "resident" population of urban casuals, winos, bums, and petty criminals. Chicago was the undisputed capital for hoboes, located as it was in the heart of the country, where it served as the hub for all the major railroads. And within the city, West Madison Street—just outside the Loop—became the mecca for hoboes.

The city offered shelter, of a wretched sort as we shall see, and, more importantly, it also provided recruiters for work. Chicago was the great labor exchange for migratory workers. The stores and walls of West Madison Street—the "main stem"—were plastered with posters offering marvelous opportunities to join a track-laying gang or other jobs. The city itself provided menial jobs, part-time and miserably paid. These were usually taken by "the home guard," Nels Anderson's felicitous term for the older hobo who could no longer sustain the rigors of riding the trains. And the city offered some badly needed medical care—almost all the hoboes were sick or hurt, and the city hospitals and dispensaries were quite familiar with hoboes and their health problems.

The shelter system was stratified. At the bottom stood the flophouses where for a pittance one could sleep on the floor or on board bunks. A flop was dry and sometimes warm, but had little else to offer. Many flophouses were associated with missions; they were a curious blend of commerce and philanthropy. A step up from the flop was the twenty-five-cent hotel, followed by the forty-cent hotel, and finally, by the elite lodging house that might have cost as much as seventy cents a night and whose guests wore collars.[31] These were clearly for the better class of workingmen. Shabbiness, both in the appearance of the lodgers and in the physical amenities of the facility, decreased as one went up the hierarchy of accommodation. The "barrel-house" was a combination rooming house, saloon, and brothel, not at all unlike the western hotel of cowboy towns. In the barrel-houses and flophouses theft was commonplace; "hold on to your possessions while you sleep or lose them" was the rule.

Movement from one accommodation to another was rapid and unidirectional; the barrel-house, with its expensive distractions, was dear. Except for the more stable workmen, the fall from the seventy-cent hotel to the flophouse was quick and relentless. The urban jungle's restaurants were cheap: in 1922 a plate of corned beef hash could be obtained for ten cents, and so could liver and brown gravy, baked beans, or sardines and potato salad. A better meal, say pig's snouts and cabbage, cost fifteen cents. And for the spree, which came early in the stop on Madison Street, a T-bone steak could be obtained for thirty cents.[32] When all money was gone, there was the mission where, after some hassles and perhaps a false show of conversion, the hobo could obtain soup, bread, and a flop—but not without a residue of bitterness:

> *Long haired preachers come out every night,*
> *Try to tell you what's wrong and what's right;*
> *But when asked how 'bout something to eat*
> *They will answer in voices so sweet:*

> *You will eat bye and bye*
> *In the glorious land above the sky;*
> *Work and pray, live on hay,*
> *You'll get pie in the sky when you die.*[33]

The "main stem" of Chicago, a single block of West Madison Street between Des Plaines and Jefferson streets, in 1922 had the typical array of enterprises found in analogous areas of cities across the country: six cheap restaurants, seven hotels, four clothiers of a sort, six saloons, four barber colleges, *ten* employment agencies, and a smaller number of missions, fortune-telling parlors, gambling joints, and drugstores.[34] The number of private organizations recruiting laborers for all kinds of purposes is significant; it speaks eloquently to the fact that this urban hobo jungle was a prime source of labor and that the maligned vagrant of the time was a *worker*.

But the hobo era was coming to its end. As Anderson reminds us in the introduction to the 1961 edition of his classic work, the hobo in 1922 "was on his way out."[35] The frontier was closed, the railroads were built, the ranches were fenced, the mines long since bled of their easy pickings, and the insatiable need for large armies of casual and migratory labor was sated. The hobo now became "a bum."

The urban jungle remained, but it had a new name and its inhabitants had aged. The jungle was probably in the same neighborhood and included the same kinds of commercial establishments, but now the local authorities referred to it as "skid row." The name derives from the street in Seattle that paralleled the log chute, or "skid," that the lumberjacks used to slide their cuttings down to the sawmill below on the waterfront of Puget Sound. In time the area around the "skid" became characterized by its shanties, cheap rooming houses and saloons. Somehow, in the cant of homeless men, the "road" became a "row," "skid row" became a synonym for the bottom rung of the urban social ladder, and the related term "on the skids" came to mean someone suffering from rapid economic decline.[36]

These urban enclaves of the destitute and homeless, as we have seen, had long been a characteristic of America's great and not-so-great cities. Skid rows existed in Boston, New York, Philadelphia, Chicago, and San Francisco—and they could also be found in Cincinnati, St. Louis, Kansas City, Stockton, and Sacramento. Always contiguous to the commercial centers of these cities, on the fringe of the bustling world of finance and wealth, skid row was a repository for the impoverished and the disaffiliated of all kinds. Skid row was home to a population of older misfits—urban nomads—whose universe encompassed a few square blocks. Their life revolved around critical landmarks: the flophouse, the cheap restaurants, the mission, and the saloon. The employment agency, so prominent in the "old" hobohemia, declined in numbers and importance.

Industrial technology had blossomed concurrently with the economic boom of World War I and the decade that followed. This technology had served to further differentiate the labor market. Labor was becoming more skilled and specialized. New cohorts of young people found an easier access into this more elite work force. The residuum shrank and itself formed a residue of the most difficult, the most marginal, the most troubled workers. They were joined by significant numbers of black men who flocked to the northern cities while following the scent of promised opportunity.

Skid row meant a life of hustle and hassle. Life energy was usually consumed by the tasks of finding something to eat and, when night fell, a place to sleep. Begging was one way to solve these cyclical demands; skid row's proximity to downtown and the well-off encouraged begging. With the coming of the automobile, there were windshields to be wiped clean and for the nervous and fidgety motorist trapped by a red traffic light a small coin was cheap ransom. Petty theft, too, was an opportunity; alas, the only realistic targets were likely to have as little as the hopeful thief.

Some "jobs" were still available. Handbills could be distributed, streets and bars swept, refuse consolidated and otherwise tidied up. Most skid rows had their early morning "slave markets" where groups of men could be found waiting for trucks to come along and recruit the desperate and unskilled for a variety of tasks to be done somewhere in the city. The unit of measurement for this casual work force was the *hour,* not the day, week, or month of happier times.[37]

The habitué of skid row was, by force, a vagrant and hence a misdemeanant. If he did not cause trouble the police were usually willing to let him be. But if he wandered outside the fuzzy perimeter of his ghetto and his presence in other areas of the city became offensive to its inhabitants, the police would cart him off to the city jail. Or if, within the confines of the Tenderloin or the Bowery or "the main stem," he became obstreperous or unmanageable to the merchants or the operators of the flops, the police would be called in to do their duty. Sometimes, they were needed to fetch an ambulance that might have to proceed directly to the morgue.

The primary element that connected the forces of law and order to the skid-row bum was alcohol. In the public mind residence in these areas was synonymous with alcohol abuse. Drink, to be sure, was the nemesis of these homeless folk: witness the number of bars found in their neighborhoods. All serious investigators of skid row reflect on the dominance of alcohol abuse in the lives of its citizens. But not all skid-row inhabitants abused beer, wine, or liquor; some, to the great joy of the missionaries, were teetotalers. Howard M. Bahr, one of the more responsible researchers, sums up the accumulated wisdom:

Several studies of the extent of drinking among skid row men have found that approximately one-third are heavy drinkers, another third drink moderately, and the remainder drink very little or are abstainers. Between one-third and one-fourth of the drinkers claim to be spree drinkers or periodic drinkers, but it is probable that many of them are merely heavy drinkers whose consumption is periodic because of financial or other factors. The proportion of abstainers ranges from 15 to 28 per cent. If residents who have been heavy drinkers in the past are counted along with the current problem drinkers, the resulting total includes at least half of the skid row population.[38]

Booze, then, was a serious component of skid-row life and a fulcrum about which much of that life revolved. Obtaining enough alcohol was a daily concern, but usually not as high on the list of priorities as obtaining the night's shelter—the lack of which, in the winter months, could be fatal. For the man on skid row, the *visibility* of his drinking was his greatest hazard. The mental portrait of established society paints a picture of unwashed and disheveled men congregating in the doorway or on the stoop, passing a bottle. This is not far from the truth. But where else can a homeless man drink except in public? The missions wouldn't have it nor would the better rooming house owners. People who can afford a private room, an apartment, or a house can drink in private. Their "drinking problem"—if they have one—is hidden from view. But the skid-row drinker drinks in public—and the effects of his drinking are public, too. The sprawled-out, semicomatose, and battered drunk is on the streets for everybody to see and for the police to cart away.

City jail, night court, drunk tank, county jail, hospital, and back again, revolving through the system of justice and health care—and always ending up back on the streets of skid row. This was and is the pattern for that part of the residuum cursed with the plague of alcohol.

With the Great Depression the skid rows of America's cities became more densely populated. World War II eventually absorbed a great many inhabitants of skid row, some into the armed services and others into the insatiable maw of wartime industry, where even habitual drunks could often find a job. The great expansion of the economy that continued after World War II continued to accommodate the marginal man, and the populations of skid row remained small and stable.

The bulldozers, in the name of urban renewal and the gentrification of the inner city, have mostly eliminated these old places. Skid row has become more diffuse—it is now both everywhere and nowhere.

The marginal labor force, exemplified by the hobo, provided the principal source for American homelessness for nearly a century. It seemed to be destined to shrink into insignificance. The physical site of its members, hobohemia transformed into skid row, seemed likely to disappear forever. By the late 1920s homelessness in America was a nonissue, a problem that had been solved through American genius and inexorable economic progress. Most people—if they thought about the problem of the homeless at all—thought that prosperity would end the problem forever. But they were mistaken.

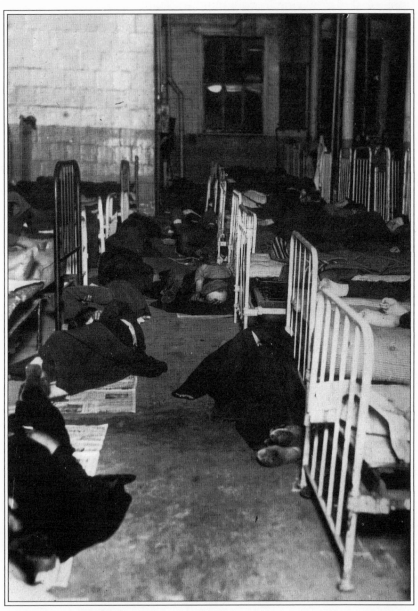

3

The Great Depression

W HAT a crash it was! The 1920s were seen by the business
and political leaders of the time as a new era—almost a
golden age. Except for farmers, who, since the end of World
War I, had had a difficult time making a go of it; and except
for a few industries, such as coal mining, the shoe industry, and
textiles; and except for that small, stable residue of tramps and
vagrants who were still at the mercy of marginal wage labor. But
for the rest of America times were good, even better than good.
The economy was expanding, employment levels were high, and
people thought that poverty would soon be eliminated. Herbert
Hoover, accepting the Republican nomination for president on
August 12, 1928, could claim: "We have not yet reached the goal,
but given a chance to go forward with the policies of the last
eight years, and we shall soon, with the help of God, be within
sight of the day when poverty will be banished from the nation."

It was the "roaring twenties," the age of the flapper and the
speakeasy, the time of the bootlegger and the gangster, of a
decade characterized by simultaneous smugness and defiance,
and a chauvinism brought on by the conduct of a successful war.
It was the time of the Palmer Raids and anti-Bolshevik hysteria;
what need had this rich and energetic country for such a foreign
ideology? America was strong; it was rich; it had unrivaled industrial power; it had won the war to end all wars and it had
saved the world for democracy.

The country was infused with the spirit of money—big money,
quick money. Speculation reached a fever pitch; deals of all kinds
were available: deals in stocks, bonds, land development, and a

host of schemes to line one's pockets. The swindles and scandals associated with the great Florida land boom hardly dented the feverish rush of speculation. Almost everyone was caught up in the excitement of wealth and prosperity. The heady brew of perpetual progress and an ever-growing economy had intoxicated the nation. The residuum seemed on the point of vanishing altogether.

The great speculative binge ended abruptly. On Thursday, October 24, 1929, the bottom dropped out of the securities market. Almost thirteen million shares were traded on the New York Exchange that day, an unheard-of volume. On the afternoon of "Black Thursday" representatives of five of the country's largest banking firms met in the boardroom of the J. P. Morgan Co. in an effort to devise a plan to stem the tide of panic selling. Thomas Lamont, senior partner of the Morgan firm, emerged from the meeting and was quoted by the *New York Times* as saying: "There has been a little distress selling on the Stock Exchange and we have held a meeting of the heads of several financial institutions to discuss the situation. . . . It is the consensus of the group that many of the quotations on the Stock Exchange do not fairly represent the situation."[1] Merrill, Lynch and Co. seized the opportunity to advise its clients "with available funds to take advantage of this break to buy good securities."[2] It is not reported what Mr. Lamont or Merrill, Lynch had to say the following week when on "Tragic Tuesday," October 29, the collapse turned into an implosion. Something on the order of nine billion dollars evaporated on that one day. From there, it was downhill for a long time. By mid-November, when the drop in security values stabilized—but only for a short while—some thirty billion dollars in paper value had disappeared—"the same amount of money America had spent on World War I."[3]

The country had seen depressions before, notably those associated with the panics of 1873 and 1893, but none had ever equaled this one in its depth, nor, as it turned out, in its duration. The Great Depression did not really end until 1941 when, spurred by a new and deadlier war, the economy recovered. Twelve years passed before this economic disaster ran its course. During those twelve years the nation experienced a hardship that put its stamp on an entire generation. For those who lived through it, even as children—perhaps especially as children—it was an ordeal never to be forgotten.

It was, at first, unbelievable. Official Washington was supremely confident that the economic downturn was temporary—a mere blip in the relentless march of economic progress. Hoover and his cabinet issued announcements of reassurance: "business could look forward to the coming year with greater assurance," proclaimed the White House at the turn of the new year. The secretary of the Treasury said quite blithely, "I see nothing . . . in the present situation that is either menacing or warrants pessimism. . . . I have every confidence that there will be a revival of activity in the spring and that during the current year the country will make steady progress."[4] In fact, business and government both saw the real menace to the country as stemming from misguided calls for *intervention* in what was believed to be a self-correcting market. Indeed, during the first few years of the Great Depression, even private charities could not bring themselves to acknowledge that the need was far beyond their capabilities. Government action, for business, was not only counterproductive but abhorrent; for philanthropy and social work it was suspect and unnecessarily intrusive.

It should not be surprising to learn that the profession of social work, newly emerged from its origins in religious sentiment and bound to the American values of individual responsibility and community self-help, would be suspicious of a large governmental role in the provision of relief.[5] But, to their credit, social workers very quickly did an about-face; they finally recognized that the need was overwhelming and far beyond the resources of private charity and the local community. Very quickly, social workers were leading a campaign calling for the federal government to do something—anything.

By 1932 the national income product had dropped to forty billion dollars from some eighty-one billion dollars three years earlier; the production of goods and services had shrunk to less than one-half of what it had been. The "land of opportunity" even saw a shift in what had heretofore been an unbroken net plus of migration; in 1932, 35,329 immigrants entered the country while over 103,000 emigrants departed for Europe or elsewhere in the hope of repairing their fortunes.[6] Some were even willing to cast their lot with the Soviet Union: AMTORG, the Soviet Union's organization for dealing with foreign trade, advertised for some six thousand skilled workers; 100,000 applied to make the journey and join the great communist experiment. Russia aside, most emigrants left America only to discover equal or worse hardship elsewhere: the depression had become worldwide. Across the face of the globe industries atrophied, factories closed.

Unemployment was the immediate personal consequence of these events, a condition for which there was no insurance. Estimates indicate that about 25 percent of the American labor force, some thirteen to sixteen million people, were out of work by 1932. These are *best* estimates; the counting of unemployed people was not yet one of the important functions of the federal government. Apart from the fact that the process of estimating unemployed people lacked precision, the periodic enumeration of unemployed people had not been perceived as a critical index of the nation's economic well-being. The whole idea of "unemployment," remember, had only recently emerged; in 1933 it was still a vague and very elastic notion.[7] Estimates derived from a variety of sources: local governments wrestling valiantly with the immediate problem, private social agencies equally enmeshed in the impossible task, and trade unions trying to find work for their members. Unemployment was an international problem: Great Britain, France, Germany, and all the other industrialized nations had no greater success either in coming to terms with the meaning of unemployment or with its magnitude.

For those still employed—and we must remember that they were in the majority, wages fell. The average weekly earnings in 1929 were thought to be above $28.50; by 1931 the average had fallen to $22.64.[8] But the fall in wages was not as rapid as the collapse in prices. This apparent prosperity for those fortunate enough to be employed was probably offset in many cases by an increase in part-time or short-time work; the rise in real wages was thus partially counterbalanced by a commensurate drop in hours worked—from forty-eight hours per week in 1929 to thirty-eight hours in the last four months of 1931.[9] Nonetheless, for certain lucky wage earners, the depression provided a long-term material benefit—although it could be argued that this plus was canceled by the anxiety and uncertainty that characterized the lives of even those who held jobs. The *psychological* costs of the depression were immeasurable for the employed as well as the unemployed.

The cities of America seemed to resemble the streets of London described by Mayhew almost a century earlier. The unemployed began to resort to hustling to secure their daily bread. A wide array of goods and services were peddled on the streets. Shoeshine "boys," charging five cents for what a few months before would have cost ten cents in shoe parlors thronged the downtown streets.

> In one block, on West Forty-third Street, a recent count showed nineteen shoe-shiners. They ranged in age from a 16-year-old, who should have been in school, to a man of more than 70, who said he had been employed in a fruit store until six months ago. Some sit quietly on their little wooden boxes and wait patiently for the infrequent customers. Others show true initiative and ballyhoo their trade, pointing accusingly at every pair of unshined shoes that passes.[10]

Cheap neckties, rubber balls, shoelaces, combs, pins, pencils, and ribbons all found an outlet through desperate entrepreneurs besieging passers-by on busy street corners. The selling of newspapers, particularly the Sunday editions, became a science: avoiding the traditional intersections and finding side streets to exploit, or moving from door to door among the apartment houses, the ingenious "newsboy" might make as much as $1.50 on a Sunday. Enterprising truck farmers from New Jersey would bypass the early morning produce market and proceed directly to neighborhoods in order to hawk their vegetables. The huddled figure of the man selling apples, often a veteran of World War I, became the national symbol of despair and hopelessness.

Begging, a behavior that had long been seen as an action characteristic of the unregenerate tramp or bum, became widespread. The panhandler was celebrated in the bitter songs of the times:

> *Once I built a railroad, made it run,*
> *Made it race against time.*

Once I built a railroad,
Now it's done—
Brother can you spare a dime?

Once I built a tower, to the sun.
Brick and rivet and lime,
Once I built a tower,
Now it's done—
Brother can you spare a dime?

Once in khaki suits,
Gee, we looked swell,
Full of that Yankee Doodle-de-dum,
Half a million boots went sloggin' thru Hell,
I was the kid with the drum.

Say don't you remember, they called me Al—
It was Al all the time.
Say don't you remember I'm your pal—
Brother, can you spare a dime?

E. Y. Harburg wrote those lyrics to what became the anthem of the depression, because—so he claims—"The prevailing greeting at that time, on every block you passed, by some poor guy coming up, was: 'Can you spare a dime?' Or: 'Can you spare something for a cup of coffee?' "[11]

The anecdotal literature on the Great Depression is full of pathetic vignettes of recently proud and industrious people, once comfortable wage earners or shopkeepers, reduced to begging and scavenging for food. Unlike the spirit invoked by the song, though, the beggar's state of mind was usually colored by shame rather than indignation. The failure of the depression years to generate any lasting political unrest in the United States was striking, as we shall see. Like those around him and surely like those who spoke for government, the panhandler saw what he did as an acknowledgment of personal defeat rather than as a sign of economic victimization. Begging was dishonorable; it had always been so. To beg was to make a clear and open announcement of failure; it was a public advertisement of one's inability to stand alone, and a testament to degradation.

The cities of America, unable to ignore this victim of hard times, rediscovered the breadline and the soup kitchen to keep him alive. There was, until the legislation of the New Deal, no federal aid of any significance; local communities tried to help but their funds were not equal to the task. Private philanthropy, organized to help the few, was unable to provide relief for the many. An emergency, ad hoc effort was the best that could be done to provide food for the hordes of people who were hungry and even starving. The old form of mission meal, stripped of its religious and moral injunctions, was expanded and dispensed from canteen or storefront. For many communities, such simple relief was all that the combined effort of local government and private philanthropy could muster. The lines formed early and ran long. They were usually notable for the silence that comes of shame.

A very large segment of the labor force had become marginal men and women. And like their counterparts of past centuries they indulged in all the techniques and devices of survival with which we are now familiar. They begged, they hawked, they scavenged, and every now and then they drifted into petty crime. And, of course, they became homeless, they moved about, and they became vagrant. Unlike his or her predecessor the hobo, however, the transient of the Great Depression had few prospects for work at the end of his or her journey. He or she was more like the sturdy beggar of Stuart times than like the migratory laborer of the fading frontier.

In the past a man looking for land, work, or new opportunities had usually headed west. But the movement of masses of Americans across the face of the country during the Great Depression did not follow the same patterns of earlier times. Movement was more random, usually governed by misinformation and rumor about opportunities for work in the next town or county or state. Although the west and southwest still exerted a magnetic attraction, nearly as much travel east as west took place. New York was a popular destination, and so was Florida.

Many communities, indeed whole states, tried to deal with the vagrant problem by turning vagrants away or by driving them out. Settlement laws, embedded in the fabric of welfare law and

policy, governed the treatment of the vagrant. Indeed, as the
magnitude of transiency increased and as the capacity to cope
diminished, the laws of settlement became more restrictive. The
state of California, for example, raised its residency requirement
in 1931 from one to three years and Colorado raised its requirement from sixty days to six months.[12] Settlement was a system
that enabled the authorities to expel strangers; but it also enabled
the bona fide resident to claim aid—such as it was—because he
or she belonged.

Like relief of any kind during these first years of the depression, the responsibility for transients was felt to be a *local* problem. Thus, at first, local solutions were invoked. The federal
government, through the Department of Commerce, circulated
literature on the care of transients to local communities. "Twenty
thousand copies of the National Association of Travelers Aid
Societies' pamphlet entitled *A Community Plan for Service to Transients* were offered to local communities 'in the belief that it may
serve as a helpful guide in dealing with the problem of transient
families.' "[13] The "plan for service" didn't help. Similar well-
intentioned tracts circulated by private organizations, such as the
Family Welfare Association of America, had comparable results.
The problem was just too big for pamphlets to solve.

The most immediately dramatic indication of homelessness
was the growth of "Hoovervilles," shanty communities that began
to appear in cities all across the country. Shelter was improvised;
pieces of discarded lumber, cardboard, scrap metal, and canvas
were employed to create makeshift homes. These flimsy structures were erected on vacant lots, under bridges or railroad els,
near town dumps, or in parks. In a spirit of enforced coopera-
tion, homeless individuals and families banded together in these
ad hoc communities where they would share "building" materials, cooking utensils, and food. New York City was the site of
several shantytowns—one, on the northern perimeter of Central
Park, was famous. Another, less notorious, Hooverville was sited
at the foot of Henry and Clinton Streets in Brooklyn, on an
abandoned dumping ground. In 1933 it was home to something
like six hundred dispossessed people and was called by its residents "Hoover City."

An insider's view of the city is provided for us by two residents, Mr. Blair, an unemployed, middle-aged machinist, and Mr. Lyon, a fifty-six-year-old seaman who, like many others in his trade, found himself abandoned and without residency rights in one of the many ports serviced by the now-depressed shipping industry. One of the most striking aspects of the stories they told was the ingenuity shown by the residents. Mr. Blair for example, originally constructed his home out of the body of a discarded truck and his bed out of two old sailor's bunks. He later added an extra room by joining a second truck body to the first. For cooking and warmth, he constructed a stove out of old pipes, iron bars, and ash cans. Mr. Lyon's place, a two-room cottage furnished with some overstuffed furniture that he salvaged from the garbage heap and repaired, and floored with some old discarded linoleum, was appropriately enough referred to by his neighbors as "The Palace." Topsoil carted from a vacant lot provided the bed for a vegetable garden he cultivated outside his door. Others similarly improvised their own homes and implements and a community grew.[14]

Hoover City got its water from a hydrant on Columbia Street, its food from scrounging, hustling, and—at times—the charity of neighbors, and its organization from the informal rules that invariably evolve in such settings. The police kept watch but did not interfere. Hoovervilles were very much like the hobo jungles of earlier decades—but without the proximity to railroads and with a relatively permanent population. For most inhabitants, they were not way stations; rather they were destinations.

The most famous of tent cities, though, was short-lived and was erected at the very edge of the nation's capital, on the far side of the Anacostia River just across the 11th Street bridge. In the summer of 1932, 25,000 unemployed and penniless veterans, many with their families, congregated in Washington, D.C., to petition their government for the soldiers' bonus promised them by a grateful Congress, but not to be paid until the year 1945. The veterans argued that they needed their money now. Anacostia was the largest encampment, but other satellite communities were scattered throughout the city. The one most noxious to officials was located on Pennsylvania Avenue within sight of

the Capitol itself. The horde of despairing men called themselves
the B.E.F., the "Bonus Expeditionary Force"; the newspapers
preferred the name "Bonus Army" or the "Bonus Marchers."

The unsightly mass of veterans terrified the city and the
nation. "Hoover Locks Self in White House" screamed the New
York *Daily News;* barricades were indeed erected around the
presidential domicile and traffic was shut down for a distance of
one block on all sides. Congress rejected the veterans' petition,
so they turned to Herbert Hoover for succor. He did not respond. The newspapers roared mightily about the "red menace"
that held the capital hostage. Congress offered to pay the veterans' fares "home"; some five thousand accepted the offer and
quietly left. The rest, equally quietly, remained. It had been, in
fact, a very decorous and peaceful assemblage of people without
a hint of violence or depredation throughout those long summer
weeks. Nonetheless, on July 28, 1932, the real army was called
in to end the matter.

General Douglas MacArthur led four troops of cavalry, four
companies of infantry, a machine gun squadron, and six tanks,
plus assorted policemen, Secret Service men, and Treasury agents.
MacArthur, ably assisted by George Patton and Dwight Eisen-
hower, led this force up Pennsylvania Avenue and across the
river, shooting, gassing, and burning. The result? Two veterans
of World War I were shot to death, scores were injured, and
hundreds were gassed. The tents and shanties were torched; the
demoralized B.E.F. left the city. "Thank God," said President
Hoover, "we still have a government that knows how to deal with
a mob." The crisis was over. But not without a public aftertaste
of bitterness, shock, and revulsion at the actions of an unfeeling
government. Hoover would surely have lost the forthcoming
election anyway; the country was sick of him. The brutal rout of
the Bonus Marchers ensured his defeat.

The tent communities of the Bonus Army, however, were an
aberration. For the most part Hoovervilles were simply places to
be lived in, not the encampments of people promoting a specific
political cause. They sprang up all over the country and were
not uniquely a cosmopolitan phenomenon—although it was in
the cities that they were most visible and attracted the most attention. Meanwhile, the traditional hobo's jungle did not dis-

appear; indeed, they grew in numbers and size as enormous numbers of new people took to the roads.

It was, in fact, youthful nomads spawned by the depression that first captured the attention of citizens and officials alike. The United States Children's Bureau, in 1932, estimated that some 200,000 boys were on the loose; other estimates ran as high as one-half million.[15] They were very visible to the railroads: D. O'Connell, in charge of the Southern Pacific's integrity, testified that fully 75 percent of the 683,457 people ejected from his trains in 1932 were between sixteen and twenty-five years of age.[16] Other railroad officials were equally concerned with the extreme youth of their unwanted passengers. And the private social agencies began to issue disturbing reports of wandering youth: Kansas City counted 1500 children passing through its city each day of 1933; Los Angeles revealed 1666 homeless boys in January of that year; Yuma, an important railway junction, claimed to have fed 30,000 youths in its soup kitchens during four months, but this figure must include more than the merely young.[17] The Salvation Army provided food for 2059 boys under twenty-one in the city of El Paso.[18]

Their child status aside, these migratory young people were not always met sympathetically by communities that usually had their own needy kids to care for:

> Atlanta, a natural way station of the hobo route in the South, gives thirty-day sentences in the city stockade or the chain gang— both of which are filled with degenerates—to anyone caught on a freight train within Fulton county. For this reason the city is widely stigmatized by tramps. Yet 6000 wandering boys were listed there through September, 1932.
>
> Miami is friendly but firm. The city provides the wanderer with a bathing suit and the unescorted freedom of its famous beach. Afterwards the vagrant is deported. Each day the so-called Hobo Express deposits eight or nine boys at the north line of the county with the warning that return will mean six months of road work. At New Orleans the transient swing to the South becomes the swing to the West. A study of welfare, police, and railroad records suggests that 5,000 wanderers traverse the city monthly, most of them under age, with only 500 seeking out the city's highly organized relief organizations.[19]

Images were invoked of the wandering children of postwar Germany just a few years before and, especially, of the *besprizorne,* the wolf children of the Soviet Union immediately after its civil war, who ran in packs to forage and despoil. This was, after all, America; what was happening to its children? The danger was clear: children, malleable as they were, could be socialized into a lifetime of vagrancy and crime. A generation of vagabonds was being spawned, and they were learning all sorts of abominable things—including homosexuality. This was true, of course: the youthful hobo often was taken under the protective—and exploitative wing—of an older "wolf."

The explanation for the phenomenon of so many children wandering the country followed predictable lines of argument: boys are by nature adventurous; they are easily led; the railroads and highways offered unprecedented opportunity for travel; families were disintegrating; school had lost its promise. To this list could be added the very reasonable explanation that flight spared a struggling parental nest another mouth to feed. If it were impossible to find a job at home, and it was, the caring youth who wanted to help his parents might take to the road and look for work elsewhere.

Girls, too, took to the road—not very many in comparison to boys but enough to make a mark on what had, historically, been an almost exclusively male fraternity. The vagrant girl could suffer even more horrible misadventures than her brother.[20]

Despite the public and official attention focused on youth, most transient and homeless people were adults, albeit young adults. The most reliable figure derives from a survey done over three days in January 1933. Social agencies in 809 cities of the forty-eight states were asked to conduct a census of their homeless. Organizations such as the Travelers Aid Society, the Salvation Army, the Y.M.C.A. and the Y.W.C.A., the National Urban League, the Family Welfare Association, and the Association of Community Chests and Councils were among those that responded to the inquiry of the National Committee on the Care of the Transient and Homeless. On the basis of these counts, an estimated national total of 1,500,000 were determined to have been homeless or migrant during those three days. But this was not, and could not have been, a complete count.

Who were these people? Where were they going? They were the unemployed and destitute, going somewhere else to try and do better. They came from all segments of American social life and from all geographic locales. A few were well educated; college students and college graduates, foreclosed from the occupational structure by the Great Depression, took to the road. Many more had graduated from high school.

But they were not perceived as educated. It took the nation a long while to realize that the transient of the 1930s was *not* the stereotypical hobo or vagabond; some good citizens were never able to accept the fact that these more modern nomads had once been their own upstanding neighbors. Most communities, hardpressed to care for their local and more stable impoverished, greeted the newcomers with hostility. "Passing on" was the typical response and it was not always gentle. Jail was another option frequently employed; the legal apparatus had its ready-made vagrancy statutes in place since colonial days. Outside of Tucson could be found a highway sign that read: "Warning to Transients. Relief funds for local residents only. Transients, do not apply." Denning, New Mexico, had store windows plastered with signs that read: "Do not ask for relief. You can be fed and slept at jail in return for 10 days' hard labor."[21] But a few days in the local jail were not always unwelcome to weary and hungry travelers:

> Fifty-four men were arrested yesterday morning for sleeping or idling in the arcade connecting with the subway through 45 West Forty-second Street, but most of them considered their unexpected meeting with a raiding party of ten policemen as a stroke of luck because it brought them free meals yesterday and shelter last night from the sudden change in the weather.[22]

The problem was obviously national in scope and required a national policy. It finally came with Franklin Delano Roosevelt and his New Deal.

A federal program of relief necessitated a profound change in perception. That *something different was happening* in the country was obvious. That local efforts were of no avail was equally obvious. But the old notion that the homeless transient was a victim of his own perversity was extremely difficult to dispel.

Throughout the testimony given before the Cutting Committee, named after Senator Bronson Cutting of New Mexico, who sponsored legislation for a national program to help needy transients, runs the theme of struggle in differentiating the truly worthy transient from his more despicable counterpart, the vagrant. This same problem had faced Henry Mayhew and almost everybody else who had been charged with the task of comprehending vagrancy. The sheer enormity of the depression phenomenon, however, decided the issue for Cutting's committee: need born of unemployment was the point. Although it wasn't said it was implied: if a few unworthy bums slipped through the legislation, so be it.

Two months after Roosevelt took the oath of office, Congress passed the Federal Emergency Relief Act, an omnibus bill that offered federal assistance to the relief efforts of the states. The act marked a change in how the nation viewed its social responsibility. People who had been struggling for years with the horrors of the depression were ecstatic. Relief through federal help had come at last:

> There's a new spirit in Washington—a resolution to get on with things that will count. With a set-up of experienced men, a law giving it wide powers and half a billion dollars in its pockets, the Federal Relief Administration has set out on one of the greatest tasks of mass-relief ever undertaken—to get relief through to all those helpless millions who need it, to make it decent and to make it prompt.[23]

Harry Hopkins, a social worker who had been running the relief programs in New York State, became the new administrator of the agency within which was housed the product of Senator Cuttings's work—the Federal Transients Bureau. The existence of the bureau was a landmark in the evolution of thought about transient people. It was, in itself, a bold statement that the phenomenon of transiency was a function of the economy—a recognition that the masses of people without shelter and without stability of residence were victims rather than misdemeanants. The old conviction that the homeless were miscreants was, with much reluctance and ambivalence, partially laid aside. Unfortunately, it could—and would—be easily resurrected.

At first, the administrators and ideologues of the Transients Bureau tried to draw a distinction between the migrant and the transient: the migrant was an individual who by employment habit and, perhaps, by nature worked at traditional seasonal and time-limited tasks; the transient was an individual who was traveling in search of a more permanent job. Making a distinction between the migrant and the transient was a difficult task hopelessly complicated by the prevailing laws of settlement. Furthermore, the distinction failed to account for local or resident homeless, people without shelter who nevertheless remained in their local communities. In time, a fourfold typology emerged: migratory-casual, unattached transient, local homeless, and families.

The migratory-casual person was the counterpart of the old hobo, an individual who habitually made his living by traveling from place to place and engaging in those occupations that were limited in time or seasonal in nature. We are by now well acquainted with him; he is the perennial solitary, the unattached migratory laborer who existed long before the depression years. A not atypical case history of the migratory-casual might read as follows:

> I went to Seattle and got a job as deckboy on a steamship that went to San Francisco. I got paid off there, got taken in by sights of the big city. Came to my senses, my boat had sailed. I had 5 cents left in my pocket. I spent it for a newspaper and looked through the ads. Porter wanted, restaurant. Convinced the boss I could do the work. $5 a week and board. Stayed there 10 days, had fight with cook, got fired.
>
> Got a job on a steamer to San Diego. Worked 3 months and then quit. Got a job in a family hotel in San Francisco as bellboy, stayed about 3 weeks and got fired for pulling a boner. Went back to San Diego. Left after short time. Got job in Hotel San Rafael, San Francisco, bellboy $15 per month.
>
> About this time I began to think of home for the first time. After 4 weeks I wrote home. Dad had moved to near Blaine, Washington, on 40 acres of unimproved land. Headed for home. Went to Aberdeen on a lumber schooner, Seattle on train, to Blaine on the boat.[24]

This is the biography of a young apprentice migratory-casual from the turn of the century; during the depression years he might meet with less luck, be less inclined to "pull boners" and get himself fired, and travel greater distances.

Another chronicle reads like this:

> July-October, 1932. Picked figs at Fresno, California, and vicinity. Wages 10 cents a box, average 50 pound box. Picked about 15 boxes a day to earn $1.50; about $40 a month.
>
> October-December, 1932. Cut Malaga and Muscat grapes near Fresno. Wages 25 cents an hour. Average 6-hour day, earning $1.50; about $40 a month.
>
> December, 1932. Left for Imperial Valley, California.
>
> February, 1933. Picked peas, Imperial Valley. Wages one cent a pound. Average 125 pounds a day. Earned $30 for season. Also worked as wagon man in lettuce field on contract. Contract price, 5 cents a crate repack out of packing houses; not field work. This work paid 60 cents to $1 a day. On account of weather was fortunate to break even at finish of season. Was paying 50 cents a day room and board.
>
> March-April, 1933. Left for Chicago. Stayed a couple of weeks. Returned to California 2 months later.
>
> May, 1933. Odd jobs at lawn, radios, and victrolas at Fresno. Also worked as porter and handyman.
>
> June, 1933. Returned to picking figs near Fresno.[25]

The next few months brought more of the same. It is not clear what this migrant laborer did during the hiatus between jobs; more than likely he joined the lines of the soup kitchens and lived in the lodging houses that catered to the desperate needs of the locally unemployed.

The life history of the *unattached transient,* in contrast to the migratory-casual, is one of residential stability until he is faced with the disaster of unemployment and the impossibility of finding local work. This individual took to the road, not as an act of volitional preference, but as a means to the end of finding new employment. His goal was to achieve domiciliary and occupational permanence. If luck was with him and he found work, he stayed put. The unattached transients were joined by new cohorts of young people looking for work outside of the communities in which they had been reared. Again, the ultimate goal was one of finding a permanent job.

In outward appearance, the transient looking for permanence was indistinguishable from the migratory laborer. Here is the case of John B.:

John B., age twenty-one of Georgia, was referred to the Miami transient bureau by the police station where he applied for food and shelter. He had come to Miami in the hope of obtaining employment during the winter in one of the winter resort hotels.

Mr. B. had left his father's farm in Georgia because "there was no future in farming," and had worked for a time as a machine tender in a cotton mill, and as a bell-boy in a small hotel. In the fall of 1934 he was out of work and unable to pay his room rent. He wrote his father asking permission to return to the farm but was told not to come. Mr. B. then applied for local relief, hoping to be assigned to a work relief project. He claims that he was refused relief because he was "single and could look out for himself."

At this point he decided to go to Florida where he heard the large resort hotels were in need of personnel. After an unsuccessful search for work in Palm Beach and Miami, he applied for assistance at the Miami police station, apparently not knowing of the transient relief bureaus.[26]

Another man eventually drifted into petty crime. Frank Bunce, aged twenty-five, educated and presumed secure in his position as a draftsman, found himself unemployed in 1931. After a fruitless search for work, "unwilling to be a burden to friends and relatives, and wanting to maintain some semblance of pride, he left his home town and began his two-year odyssey. Sometimes he worked briefly as an itinerant farmer, but, for the most part, his experiences were in flops, boxcars, soup lines, missions, and finally, on the streets begging."[27] He became proficient at the art of begging and became, in the jargon of the times, a "wise stiff"—a term that implied being able to create all sorts of affecting tales to offer passing marks, but also suggested a mental attitude, a conviction that it had become absolutely futile to look for anything other than mere subsistence. Small-time thievery next engaged him. In spite of his newfound skills, Mr. Bunce never learned to accept the humiliations consequent upon panhandling; he still yearned for a job, a home, and a family.

It is the first couple of weeks at tramping that hurt a man most. Added to the uneasiness of any animal in a strange environment is the human feeling of depravity from his beggar's status. One talks badly, goes hungry for unnecessarily long periods of time, walks needlessly after nightfall, goes blocks out of his way to avoid policemen. . . .

But we're not on the road by choice; it's hard compulsion. We're foraging animals in thin pastures and we have to cover an incredible lot of territory to keep alive. . . .

What, I wonder, would they have me do? Blithely chisel quarters from old schoolmates? Circulate at the back doors of people who knew your mother, and yourself when you were in rompers? Or just crawl into a hole and starve?[28]

The unattached transient was not consistently on the move; when he stopped—and he did for long periods of time—he blended in with those homeless who had never left their communities.

The local homeless consisted of the old, the sick, and the timid, and those who had become too weary to begin or to continue on a futile journey. These people had only one option: to stay put and live on the streets or in the shantytowns. Some of the local or resident homeless were leftovers from earlier days—the dregs of hobohemia and skid row. Most were newly unemployed. In both cases, life became a quest for survival: where to get a next meal, where to find a night's shelter.

These needs could be met by municipal facilities, always overstrained. New York City had one of the more generous setups:

The Lodging House opens at four in the afternoon and by that time, the line outside the door is the better part of a block long. It will be twice as long by six. One hundred twenty-eight men are admitted about every twenty-five minutes, that being the length of time it takes for one sitting in the dining room. Every man receives a cup of coffee (in a tin cup, boiling hot), a big dish of stew (beef tonight and lamb tomorrow) and as much graham bread as he can eat. Anyone capable of consuming a second helping of stew is welcome to it. After supper, they are registered and check their valuables (nine out of ten haven't any, and if by a miracle somebody turned up with three dollars he would be refused admission). Every man hands in all his clothing, to be fumigated during the night and returned to him in the morning. Every man gets a shower bath—compulsory; a clean white nightshirt, and a medical examination. If he needs a doctor's care, he is sent over to Bellevue Hospital; otherwise, he gets in bed in a room with several hundred other men, where he sleeps about eleven hours; and so would you, if you had tramped the streets from dawn to dark and had just had a big hot meal, perhaps your first in several days. The earliest men to come in are the earliest out in the morning. Each process takes several hours, when the city's guests are running above a thousand at a time. Every man gets back his clothing and valuables, the garments fumigated in dry heat, and neither wrinkled nor given any odor by the process. Once clad, they are checked out again, are given a hot breakfast, and sent on their way. A few of the men—less than 10 per cent—are required to do a couple of hours' cleaning work to pay for their lodging; the rest make no payment except the humiliation of accepting charity.[29]

No one could use this rather sumptuous facility for more than five nights in any one month; the other twenty-five days must have been spent with considerably less in the way of amenity. During the first two months of 1930 almost 14,000 men were cared for in this particular municipal lodging house.

The above three categories of homeless people informally devised by the Transients Bureau were obviously not at all static. The unattached transient could easily fall into the ranks of the migratory-casual; both of these groups contained individuals who would almost always end up among the resident homeless of any given community; and the local homeless might pick up and move. There was a constant and fluid motion among the types. Yet the categories were more or less real; the meager statistical data from the Transients Bureau bear this truth out. Thus, John Webb's analysis of data derived from the Transients Bureau reveals a predictable age distribution.[30]

One would expect the unattached transients to be, on the whole, younger than habitual migratories, considering this latter group's residual component of older hoboes; one would also expect the local homeless to be among the oldest—older people,

Table 3–1
Types of Transient Bureau Homeless by Age

Group	Median Age
Unattached transients	27–30
Migratory-casuals	37
Local homeless	42–45

Source: Adapted from data presented in John N. Webb, *The Transient Unemployed,* Works Progress Administration Research Monograph no. 3 (Washington, D.C.: U.S. Government Printing Office, 1938).

Table 3–2
Type of Homeless by Education

Education	Transient Homeless	Resident Homeless
No schooling	2.0%	6.1%
Less than 8th grade	29.8	43.2
Completed 8th grade	26.3	27.9
Attended high school	25.1	13.2
Completed high school	12.9	7.0
Attended college	2.8	1.6
Completed college	1.1	1.0
Total	100.0	100.0

Source: Adapted from John N. Webb, *The Transient Unemployed,* Works Progress Administration Research Monograph no. 3 (Washington, D.C.: U.S. Government Printing Office, 1938).

after all, would be less likely to be healthy and strong enough to hit the road. Further, the same study reveals a predictable difference between transient homeless and resident homeless in respect to their educational backgrounds. The higher educational achievement of the transients no doubt can be explained by the fact that they were younger; prior to the depression, children were staying in school for longer periods of time than their parents had.

There was a fourth group among the clientele of the Transients Bureau, however, that was essentially new to students of vagrancy: *families,* which existed in large numbers.

Migratory families were, by a large majority, traveling in hopes of finding permanent work and then establishing a new permanent home. A very few had been migratory laboring families before the depression, but these were the exceptions. In a previous era, the migratory family of the 1930s might have moved west to become settlers, but now, of course, the frontier was long gone. At first, homeless families were not perceived to be a problem of great significance; the depression migrant population was believed to consist mostly of unattached men and teenaged boys.

> The underestimation of family distress migration during the early years of the depression partly grew out of the fact that family mobility was less spectacular than the mobility of unattached persons. Needy families did not ride the freight trains or congregate at the railroad yard limits where they would have attracted attention at every town along the main-line railroads. Instead they moved largely by automobile so that, except for the general state of disrepair of their cars and the frequent protrusion of personal belongings from the sides, they differed little in appearance from many nonmigrant travelers on the highways.[31]

Further, they were prudent in their travels; most moved relatively short distances from their homes. Usually, they went to places where they were known or where they had relatives or friends to help them. They were primarily intact family units; 91 percent of the families serviced by the Transients Bureau were without absent members. And they were relatively small: two-person families accounted for 35 percent of the total and three-person families added another 25 percent. Further, the data reveal that the families were predominantly white—at least as far as the Transients Bureau's cases were concerned; black migrant families may simply not have turned up at this organization's offices. A stunning 98 percent were citizens; the migrant families, then, were more "American" than the general population.[32]

The archetype of the depression migrant family was the Okie, so dramatically portrayed by John Steinbeck in his *The Grapes of Wrath*. The language of the outraged Californians who met these travelers with barricades and state police also generated "Arkies" and "Texies." But the refugee from the Dust Bowl was a latecomer to the ranks of depression-era family migrants and contributed only a relatively small proportion of the total numbers of families who migrated during those fearsome years. The great drought of the Central Plains that ruined so many small farmers and sharecroppers did not yield its bitter harvest of family migrants until the second half of the depression. They were a dramatic but johnny-come-lately addition to the scene.

The more typical families who packed their belongings into cars or trucks were displaced by the closing of industries, the failures of small shops, or the collapse of coal mining. The following histories are illustrative.

> *Roy Harris* had been a West Virginia coal miner for 30 years. In the summer of 1934 the mine at which he had been working closed down. He was too old to get a job in another mine, and there was no hope of other work. The Harrises applied for resident relief but were unable to live on the allowance they received. Mr. Harris had a brother living in St. Louis. In the spring of 1935 Mr. and Mrs. Harris and the two children moved to St. Louis to try to locate the brother, who they thought could help them find work. When they found Mr. Harris's brother, he was unable to help them, and the family applied for transient relief.[33]

This was a single move; others were more involved.

> *William Kruger* had been working as a house painter in Chicago for 10 years. Work became harder and harder to find, and after September 1933 there was none at all. In the summer of 1934 the couple applied for relief, but while waiting for relief to be granted they were evicted from their home. On the same day, learning that a friend was preparing to drive to San Antonio, the couple persuaded him to let them go along. Mr. Kruger was unable to find work in San Antonio and the couple registered at the transient bureau. After 6 weeks they moved to Shreveport, La., where Mr. Kruger found a job driving a caravan of automobiles to Los Angeles. When they registered at the Los Angeles transient bureau, they were promptly returned to Chicago for resident relief. The Krugers were by now completely dissatisfied with Chicago. In June 1935, after 2 months in Chicago, Mr. Kruger found another job driving a caravan to San Francisco. They had been in the San Francisco

transient bureau for 3 weeks when interviewed and insisted that they would not return to Chicago. Mr. Kruger had been promised a job as a painter and the couple proposed to settle down in California.[34]

These simple, straightforward, and inelegant case histories from the records of the Transients Bureau—which served 200,000 different families containing 700,000 individuals in the course of two years—conceal more than they reveal. The sparse narrative accounts hide a great deal of pain and pathos. The eviction of the Krugers from their home is passed over, in the case record, much too quickly: the ousting of many families from homes, apartments, and farms was widely prevalent and always accompanied by the most heart-wrenching scenes.

Johannes Schmidt, a German immigrant, had successfully farmed 120 acres in Iowa for several years. The collapse in farm prices resulted in the usual escalation of indebtedness, compounded by the pressure of local banks calling in their loans because they themselves were on the verge of failure.

> This man Schmidt had struggled and contrived as long as possible under the prodding of landlord and banker, and as a last resort came to see me about bankruptcy. We talked it over and with regret reached the conclusion it was the only road for him to take. He did not have even enough cash on hand to pay the thirty-dollar filing fee which I had to send to the Federal Court but finally borrowed it from his brother-in-law. The time of hearing came, and he and his wife and children sat before the Referee in Bankruptcy, while the banker and the landlord struggled over priorities of liens and rights to crops and cattle. When the day was over this family went out from the office the owner of an old team of horses, a wagon, a couple of cows and five hogs, together with their few sticks of furniture and no place to go.[35]

Schmidt was fortunate: he was left with much more than many people who suffered the nightmare of foreclosure and eviction. Sometimes neighbors would rally to postpone the inevitable.

> This was at the time [when hogs were two cents a pound and corn was eight cents a bushel] that mortgaging of farms was

getting home to us. So they was having ten cent sales. They'd
put up a farmer's property and have a sale and all the neighbors'd come in, and they got the idea of spending twenty-five
cents for a horse. They was paying ten cents for a plow. And
when it was all over, they'd all give it back to him. It was legal
and anybody that bid against that thing, that was trying to get
that man's land, they would be dealt with seriously, as it were.[36]

Such instances, inspiring as they might have been, were few and
far between for the very simple reason that neighbors were likely
to be in much the same sea of financial trouble.

The psychological costs of the depression, and specifically
the price paid by unemployed men and women, did not go un-
noticed. It was obvious to the researchers of those forlorn times
that squalor, eviction, impoverishment, begging, homelessness,
and transiency would leave their mark on the personality. The
loss of a job might at first generate a fever of activity to find
another, but the job search itself often ended in apathy. One of
the earlier studies of the human costs of the depression was
conducted in London, where the progression on the road to
despair was described by a victim. Three days after being laid
off, he was confident: "there's plenty of jobs for a man with my
experience." Three weeks later, he was discouraged but still
hopeful. After five weeks he is losing faith in himself: "I'm beginning to wonder what's wrong with me." Eight weeks later he
is depressed: "Either I'm no good, or there is something wrong
with business around here. . . . even my family is beginning to
think I'm not trying." Finally, after four months, he is utterly
despondent, and mentions "the hopelessness of every step you
take."[37]

P. F. Lazarsfeld, in a study of an Austrian community, found
four types of victim: "about half he classified as resigned to their
fate; they had learned to accept a circumscribed existence, had
no plans or expectations. Another quarter he called despairing—
these were bitter, gloomy, frequently drunk, given to outbursts
of misdirected rage. Another, smaller group were completely
apathetic, heedless not only of the future but even of the present.
Only about 16 percent of these people could be classified as
'unbroken' and they, significantly, had higher incomes than the

rest."[38] Defeatism, passivity, numbness, and deep shame were the typical responses to the catastrophe of sudden, unexpected, and then prolonged unemployment. That mental set serves to explain—to the chagrin of radicals—the inability of most sufferers to join in any telling political activity.

But the above descriptions are not psychiatric conceptions; American studies, conducted by bona fide psychologists and psychiatrists, were more clinical in their language. "Anxiety" was manifest; "psychosis" was evident; indeed, "Many of the respondents displayed a 'catastrophic' outlook toward life and were as 'downcast' as mental patients."[39] Many victims of unemployment turned to alcohol for relief from their pain. The sum total of the experience was perhaps best expressed by a victim of unemployment half a century earlier in London: "Whenever I am out of work I feel like a bloody dog."[40]

The question of whether the transient homeless were people predisposed to that condition by virtue of their precarious mental status or whether their psychological condition derived from the experience of unemployment and homelessness was partially answered by these various studies. The latter formulation seemed to be more compelling in regard to the depression-era dispossessed: people who had been gainfully employed, who had lived in settled residences, and who had been psychologically stable *became* deeply troubled by what had happened to them. Their psychological state was made manifest in their behavior: listlessness, inattention, drinking, petty crime, mendicancy, and a pervasive apathy and resignation. They had become, in fact, mentally disturbed. Of course, some of them might have had problems prior to the catastrophe of the depression; but such predispositions were masked by their ability to "make it" in a benign labor market. When that external employment market turned hostile, their propensities emerged to become more overt, handicapping, and perhaps even dominant.

The Federal Transients Bureau was brought into existence in order to meet the pressing need of those without local residence. The program took different forms in different states. One of the more prevalent forms was the transient "camp" located in the nonurban areas of a state. There, residents would be housed (sometimes in tents), fed, schooled, and frequently trained for some supposed future employment. They would be put to work: mending and building roads, maintaining other public facilities such as parks and recreation centers, and keeping up the camps themselves. These camps were, in some significant respects, similar to those of the Civilian Conservation Corps (C.C.C.), but without the military coloration or the latter's involvement in reforestation. Other Transients Bureau devices were comparable to the city shelter or hostel; still others were essentially referral and information centers; and some styled themselves as "rehabilitation" units.

Throughout its brief existence, the Transients Bureau was plagued by the familiar and very stubborn conviction, held by the community at large, that transients were dangerous degenerates. Whenever a problem occurred within the camps and shelters and was reported in the local newspapers, there would be a predictable outcry of indignation. Most of these incidents revolved around drink: "The arrest of one transient for vagrancy or alcoholism did more to shape community attitudes than the behavior of 100 men working 30 hours a week on community projects."[41] Reports of theft and, every once in a while, more heinous incidents such as murder or rape generated frantic outrage. At another level, there was even a touch of envy in the critique:

> To the stay-at-home, confronted with unescapable problems of his own, the life of a transient, free from the responsibilities of settled life, frequently appeared at once glamorous and reprehensible. This romantic attitude obscured an understanding of the economic and social problems in which the transient was involved. So long as he was regarded as a cross between a carefree gypsy and a fugitive from justice, a reasonable approach to his quandary was impossible.[42]

Many people actually believed that the programs of the Transients Bureau were somehow making life much too easy for transients—that the life of vagrancy was essentially being encouraged by the camps and shelters.

Some, more thoughtful, people believed that depression-era transiency could be mitigated in its individual effects by the Transients Bureau, but that the essential problem was intractable because it was embedded in the larger economic disturbance. Until a more general solution could be found for the unemployment or subemployment of people, homelessness would remain. Such a solution, it was felt, had begun to appear in the modest economic recovery of 1935–36—a recovery that proved to be illusory. Further, the Roosevelt administration began a slow retreat from its policy of direct relief to the victims of the depression— a bold and uncharted experiment that had provoked the fear and wrath of many. The Transients Bureau's days were numbered; an unprecedented endeavor that, for the first time in American history, had taken as its basic principle of operation that the homeless were suffering victims worthy of humane and decent treatment, was coming to an end.

In September 1935 the program was severely curtailed. The states were notified that no more persons were to be accepted for transient's relief. The administration had proposed a daring new Social Security Act and a vast program of public works that would substitute work relief for direct relief. The newly created Works Projects Administration (W.P.A.), with Harry Hopkins as director, absorbed many who had been on the rolls of the Transients Bureau. The homeless were no longer to be separated out from the larger population of needy for a special attention. Those with "residence" would be put to work; those without residence, however, were to become once again the forgotten and the despised. The inanity of defining a "worthy" transient in terms of his intransiency returned to its awkward place in welfare theory.

The Great Depression ended with the carnage of World War II. Many young men were absorbed into the vast armies and navies that were being mustered. Those who were left usually found jobs in a booming wartime economy. At war's end the United States was the dominant economic power of the planet. Many felt that the problem of unemployment was essentially over, and that the transient and homeless would soon become a memory. Except for the hopeless dregs of skid row, cursed by alcohol abuse, the homeless man and woman was no more. And except, too, for the occasional young person intoxicated with the misguided spirit of adventure and wanderlust.

4

Antinomians and "Free Spirits":
The Hippies

THE shaping force of economy made manifest in the vicissitudes of wage labor—powerful as it is—cannot explain
all transient and homeless behavior.[1] Humankind has other needs,
and catastrophe can be a state of mind as well as a material
condition. So it has been with recurrent outbreaks of social
expression captured by such conceptions as antinomianism, mil-
lenarianism, bohemianism, and romanticism. It is surely a perversion of both the historical record and reality to lump the many
diverse social, political, and religious movements embraced by
these notions into one supercategory. But common threads bind
their disparities: they all arise in periods of cultural crisis; they
share a rejection of and contempt for orthodoxy; for the most
part, they celebrate the primacy of the free and unencumbered
spirit; and they frequently exalt the virtues of poverty and simplicity. For the poor, who contributed the greatest numbers to
most of these causes, the glorification of poverty was an act of
self-exaltation.

The most stunning modern example of such a movement
was our own hippie phenomenon of the late 1960s.[2] Hippiedom
was short-lived, as many such movements are, but the phenomenon attracted a great flurry of popular attention and generated
excitement while it lasted. It also stimulated a mountain of jour-
nalistic and even scholarly nonsense. As we proceed to consider
some of the antinomian predecessors of the hippie it will be

instructive to hold in mind the events of San Francisco's Haight-Ashbury district with its armies of flower children.

The great binding force of Western civilization has been, until very recently, the church, so it is not surprising that most of the past crusades for spirit and selfhood were religious in nature. Some of them were, *in fact,* Crusades. Almost all these movements were condemned as heresy by the upholders of orthodoxy. Adherents of these social movements invoked the model set by Christ and his Apostles, and condemned wealth and comfort. They became mendicant wanderers who forsook material comforts for the ecstasy of spirit. Thus Christ's life as reported in the New Testament often proved embarrassing to what had evolved into a very wealthy and often too material mother church.

The antinomians believed that moral law based on the teachings of the church was incomplete; the inner self, the divine soul was an alternate, or even the only true, source of revelation. The Gnostics, the heretical bane of the early church, believed that true "knowing" was the issue; the Gnostic sects rejected knowledge based on reason and cognitive processes and substituted the greater truths derived from personal revelation, intuition, illumination, and vision—whether self-induced or prompted by substance.

> These movements [the Gnostics] rejected the worldly life and turned to the interior self for truth. Scorning established institutions, they insisted on direct and personal access to insight and to God. They defended faculties that they deemed to be superior to reason and to order. Liturgy and ritual had lost meaning for them. They reached out for a pantheistic fusion and unity or for a total escape from the bondage of this evil world. The members of these sects founded utopian communities and colonies and aspired to a self-actualization in which they would free the pneuma, or spirit, from its bondage in the contemptible body. They spoke in tongues, joined cults of love, and sought ecstasy as a steady state.[3]

Shades of Marshall McLuhan and Timothy Leary! Some gnostics sought knowledge through license, others through asceticism, but all lived a life characterized by simplicity and derision for the establishment.

Manichaeans, a Gnostic-like sect of the early church, practiced an exotic and ritualized diet that they hoped would bring on visions. "They roamed the countryside as wanderers, beggars, and vagabond preachers. Pacifists, they repudiated killing animals. They refused to work or to comply with secular regulations and lived instead on charity."[4] The Manichaeans did not survive their condemnation by the church but their name remained as a generic term for similar movements that arose during the Middle Ages.

That era, haunted by dark and foreboding specters of apocalypse, provoked an amazing array of antinomian movements: Bogomils, Cathars, Patarenes, Albigensians, Waldensians, Flagellants, and others arose, struggled for acceptance by the forces of religious respectability, and either fizzled out of their own accord or were ruthlessly suppressed. Some were passive in stance, others militant; some were meek, others disobedient; a few seemed to be nothing more than cults of pranksters or the outrageous.

The Beghards, of the late thirteenth and fourteenth centuries, from which the English word *beggar* is supposed to derive, are an interesting instance. In some regions they were also known as the Lollards.

> They frequented towns and ranged through the streets in noisy groups, shouting for alms and crying their characteristic begging-cry: "Bread for God's sake!" They wore costumes rather like those of the friars, yet specially designed to differ from these in certain details. Sometimes the robe was red, sometimes it was split from the waist down; to emphasize the profession of poverty the hood was small and covered with patches. The Beghards were an ill-defined and restless fraternity—running about the world, we are told, like vagabond monks. . . .
>
> Some of them had no fixed abode at all, would carry nothing on their persons, refused to enter any house and insisted on staying in the street to eat whatever food was given them. And—again like the rest of the "voluntarily poor"—they included people of very varied social antecedents.[5]

Many Beghards came from the great mass of poor, but there were also a significant number of artisan workers as well as some adherents from the "less privileged strata of the intelligentsia," or clerics of the minor monastic orders. Literacy, a rare attainment in medieval European society, was more common among the Beghards and Lollards. They were the true free spirits of the age, emphatically rejecting the bondage of material possession. They preached that the spirit within rather than the dogma and authority of the church was the source of true godliness.

But it was during the great personal excitement and disorientation of England during the throes of its civil war that movements, more similar to the hippies of 1967, were produced. The *original* Diggers of 1650 formed a community in Surrey, England, wherein private property, class distinction, and human authority had no place. Their name derived from the digging of common fields in which their food was cultivated. The Diggers hoped to restore mankind to its original pristine, simple, and innocent state. We shall see the Diggers reappear in the panhandle of Golden Gate Park.

Another English movement, the Ranters, were more energetic in their vision of a sublime selfhood. Sin itself became a great lie foisted upon humankind by the despicable system:

> [They taught that] God regardeth not the Actions of the Outward Man, but the Heart; and that to the Pure all things are Pure, (even things forbidden): And so as allowed by God, they spoke most hideous Words of Blasphemy, and many of them committed Whoredoms commonly: Insomuch that a Matron of great Note for Godliness and Sobriety, being perverted by them, turned so shameless a Whore, that she was Carted in the streets of London.[6]

To the Ranters, *all* that was human was divine—God was everywhere, everyone was God:

> Some say, nothing is unclean to us, no not sin; we can commit any sin, for we esteem not any thing to be unclean, but those that do, to those it is a sin. . . . We are pure, say they, and so all things are pure to us, adultery, fornication, etc. we are not defiled. . . . If God be all things, then he is sin and wickedness; and if he be all things, then he is this Dog, this Tobacco-pipe, he is me, and I am him, as I have heard some say.[7]

Alan Watts could not have put it more neatly.

Monogamy, too, was often seen as an invention of stultifying orthodoxy. The promiscuity of the crash pad had its precursor some three hundred years ago: "They say that for one man to be tyed to one woman, or one woman to one man, is a fruit of the curse; but they say, we are freed from the curse; therefore it is our liberty to make use of whom we please."[8] The blasphemy and provocatively foul language of Ranters cannot help but remind us of the Filthy Speech Movement, Berkeley's short-lived follow-up to the Free Speech Movement of 1964, and of its irrepressible spokesperson, Jefferson Fuck Poland, who had the audacity—or genius—to want to take that name *legally*. The idea, in part, was to *shock;* the Ranters succeeded admirably. The economic and political posture of the Ranters also resembled the anarcho-communism of the hippie. Private property was a joke: "That they should borrow money, and never pay it again; and that they should not only make use of a Man's Wife, but of his Estate, Goods and Chattels also, for all things were common."[9]

The "free spirit" celebrated in these several millenarian movements implied a life of poverty and necessitated a very tenuous attachment to domesticity and permanence of residence. The earth, itself, became one's abode; the human being would be at home anywhere wherever he found himself. Millenarian adherents, then, could hardly be distinguished in appearance from the armies of secular beggars and homeless who roamed the face of the European continent.

It remained for the romantics to interject the idea of unadulterated *joy* into the free spirit; millenarians were too bogged down in the morass of theology and too preoccupied with a forthcoming Day of Judgment to really indulge in an earthly ecstasy. Antinomianism broke free from such unhappy ruminations in the late eighteenth and early nineteenth centuries and became secular. We call this new, secular form of antinomianism *romanticism,* the cultural movement that grew out of the social chaos wrought by early industrialization, the French Revolution, and the Napoleonic wars. Like the antinomians, though, the romantics emphasized imagination, intuition, and vision rather than cognitive processes. Intensity of experience rather than its comprehension was the goal sought:

> The romantic craved sensation, made a cult of awareness, and hones his appetite for the exotic and the macabre. He sought emotion for emotion's sake, explored the extravagant, exper-

imented with obscure and violent feelings, and found special truths in madness and in polymorphous perversions. . . . the romantic, spiritual, or physical tourist sought periods and places that are extraordinary and exotic, where habits were likely to be strange or horrible, and motives passionate and unusual. The romantic reasserted the primacy of intuitive, emotional, and inspirational values. He renewed the quest for that fusion, enthusiasm, and "organic" unity of which he had been deprived by Newton's image of the universe.[10]

New fashions of weeping and swooning, of dress, a deification of primitive and folk art, and a zeal for the values of the simple, rural peasant became part and parcel of romantic sensibility. The ancestors of the hippies in the 1820s and 1830s, in France, took the form of the romantic *les Bouzingos:*

> Their hair [was] brushed up from the sides into a high peak to simulate the flame of genius. In place of a waistcoat, some wore black velvet, tightly fitting doublets and loose jackets with wide velvet lapels, and black flowing ties. Others dressed like Spanish grandees, in Cossack boots, or in bright blue frock coats with gold buttons like those worn by an Indian Maharaja. Still others wore sweeping light blue coats lined with pale pink and fastened by pearl buttons as large as our half dollar.
>
> They played at dandyism, nudism, Satanism; they used drugs such as stramonium, belladonna, and atropine to dilate their pupils and to achieve a look of strange fixity. They assumed roles either of intense passion or of impassivity and detached coolness.[11]

Their dance was frenetic, voluptuous, and rhythmic—like that of the witch's Sabbath. It was to evolve, soon, into the cancan, whose original form was much less subdued than that found today in the tourist haunts of Montmartre. The music, the posture, the apparel, the outrageous contempt for convention, the drugs—all were to be seen later in the streets of San Francisco during the summer of 1967.

Les Bouzingos evolved into the bohemianism that has remained part of the fabric of all cosmopolitan life. The bohemians, although they may have been born into bourgeois homes, became poor, of course: note only the struggling Rudolfo, his ragged friends, and the consumptive Mimi of *La Boheme*.[12] Their poverty was no less real because it was self-imposed. Bohemians could be said to have lived by an implicit system of rough and rather loose ideas that bound them together and separated them from the larger society. Bennet Berger summarizes these canons of bohemian life. Remember, these are the tenets of a nineteenth-century bohemianism:

—The idea of salvation by the child. In short, it is the notion of innocence and self-actualizing potential. If left alone by the corrupting and crippling forces of convention, the child personality, intrinsically wise, would prevail.

—The idea of self-expression. Or, in the jargon of the 1960s, "do your own thing." All expression, if authentic, is not only real but valuable.

—The idea of paganism. The body is a temple, inherently clean and immaculate and a "shrine to be adorned with the ritual of love."

—The idea of living for the moment. The postponement of experience and pleasure for some indefinite and more than likely fictitious future is a perversion of nature.

—The idea of liberty. This is in respect to a personal liberty: "every law . . . that prevents self-expression or the full enjoyment of the moment should be shattered and abolished. Puritanism is the great enemy." It is not surprising that this liberty would often include a political component, but frequently politics was beside the point.

—The idea of female equality. Women now appear on the stage as significant actors.

—The idea of mystic insight, helped along by chemical substance if necessary. For the bohemians of nineteenth-century Paris, such substances included belladonna, opium, and absinthe.

—The old romantic ideal of love of the exotic. "The idea of changing place. They do things better in . . . (you name it)."[13]

We shall see, as you have already probably begun to perceive, that the hippie shared these doctrines of the free spirit and added many refinements and embellishments of his or her own. Bohemian or romantic life was, at times, inseparable from the lifestyles of large numbers of students all over continental Europe. The notion of an unfettered freedom for the chosen elect reached its extreme point in Dostoyevsky's portrait of Raskolnikov in *Crime and Punishment.* Believing himself unbound by conventional morality—indeed, *entitled* and even enjoined to do anything so as to further his potential—Dostoyevsky's character was the apotheosis of the free spirit collectively anticipated by the Ranters and embodied, with some temper, by the romantics. And, perhaps, the genius of Gauguin was a prime example of the romantic elevation of the noble primitive to a perfection of experience and living. Tahitians were *real;* bourgeois Parisians were the nineteenth-century equivalent of plastic.

The calamity of industrialization and urban growth had a deep effect on the children of newly formed burghers. We have seen what these events had done to the working classes; the sons and daughters of the middle classes were disoriented in a different way. Their privilege became an empty promise; what did it all mean and what was it all worth?

Thus were born the *Wandervögel* of Central Europe, the "wandering birds" who traipsed the countryside with pack and staff on a quest for the authentic life.

> The original Roamers *[Wandervögel]* seemed to have been primarily romantic rebels, not self-conscious advocates of a new "youth culture". . . . The pattern was that of prolonged truancy or vagrancy, accompanied by more than a little rowdyism. . . . Costume was highly individualized and sometimes approached the rags and tatters of the quasi-mythical "wandering scholar" of medieval times or the nondescript, dirty garb of the "raggle-taggle Gypsies, O!" . . . Alcoholic drinks were freely indulged in on occasion, and smoking was not barred. Still further, there may have been a good deal of *Shickserei,* i.e. the casual picking up of servant girls, daughters of itinerant artisans such as coopers and tinkers, and occasionally, when nights were spent in haystacks or peasants' dwellings in remoter regions, the surviving remnants of old-fashioned bundling may have proved congenial.[14]

By the early twentieth century the *Wandervogel* could be found trudging all over northern Germany and Brandenburg, sometimes in tattered, raggedy garb, which was usually bedecked with colorful and fluttering ribbons; backpacks carried their few belongings and lutes and guitars were slung across their shoulders for the evenings' songs around the campfires.

> They too sought the whole man, banded together and improvised rituals, sought a vigorous life and blood brotherhood, and set out upon a trip, a quest . . . [they] found their anchorage in a pantheistic union with nature. In a deranged world, the search for meaning and purpose reinstates the first god— the tribe. . . .
>
> Like contemporary mimes and guerilla theater, players toured the countryside, presenting both popular and mystery plays. These groups sought, as the "new theater" does today, to break out of the proscenium and to create a unity between players and audience. First the youth movement called for "the convalescence of nature" to overcome the sickness of civilization. Later, a large part of the prewar *Wandervogel* ultimately turned to political action.[15]

Unfortunately, the politics that many turned to was that of National Socialism. Before their descent into the abyss of Hitlerism, however, the adherents immersed themselves in a life of vagabonding through the Alps, wallowing in folk culture, exalting the primitive, and playing with promiscuity and homosexuality.

The culmination of the *Wandervogel* movement was a great happening—the Meissner Fest—held in October 1913 on Mt. Meissner. A new age was announced to the world, one, alas, that was to be aborted by the events of the following August. "Some sought a mass migration out of the cities or to the Orient, while others sought a 'secession of all those of good will' to begin building an ideal 'natural' life of farming and craft settlements."[16] Meissner was really the end of the *Wandervogel* movement, just as Woodstock was to become both an apogee and a terminus for the age of Aquarius.

America's new world was not announced by its free spirits until January 1967 at the great human "be-in" held in San Francisco's Golden Gate Park. Prior to that time the Haight-Ashbury district had been a neighborhood unique to San Francisco. One of the few areas to escape the destruction of the 1906 earthquake, it became quite fashionable in the years that followed, and was a locus for the carriage trade. But as the city grew and sprawled, less affluent people began to enter the community such that, during and after World War II, a rather special heterogeneity of race and social class became characteristic of the Haight-Ashbury. By the time of the neomillenarian events about to unfold, it had already been a neighborhood characterized by tolerance and social experimentation for several decades.

Throughout the 1950s and early 1960s a combination of mild urban deterioration and absentee landlords led to relatively low rents. Low rents made the area attractive to many different kinds of people whose low incomes would otherwise have prevented them from living in a community with the natural amenities of the Haight-Ashbury. Moreover, the district was close to several of the city's important educational centers: San Francisco State College, the University of San Francisco, and the University of California Medical Center. Thus the prehippie Haight-Ashbury had already become a mixture of stable working-class people, upwardly mobile blacks, established (if slightly offbeat) professionals, students, some of their instructors, and a few remnants of the old bohemia and the last of the Beat generation who had been driven from their North Beach haunts by the new tourist craze of topless bars and clubs. The decimated Beats were to provide a rather befuddled and hesitant artistic voice to the "movement"; they also provided a name. The new young folk of the Haight-Ashbury were condescendingly called, by these elders, "hipsters," a term quickly transformed into "hippies."

In spite of this variegated population, the neighborhood had a remarkable spirit of cohesion. This harmony found an organizational expression in the Haight-Ashbury Neighborhood Council (HANC), a consortium of homeowners, tenants, and other residents who looked with pride upon their neighborhood. HANC was unusual; in the days before community participation was even known as such, the organization successfully mobilized itself to fight off a planned superexpressway that would have extended into Golden Gate Park and destroyed the park panhandle. HANC was tolerant and predisposed to welcome the exuberance and outlandish behavior of what became known as the flower child.

By long tradition, then, the neighborhood accepted diversity. The hippie movement could not have found a more accepting environment. It had a thriving homosexual community, so much so that, according to an apocryphal story, a local motion picture theater, long closed, was reopened as the Straight Theater in 1967 to announce to the community at large that heterosexuals were also welcome. The physical characteristics of the Haight-Ashbury, bounded on the north by the panhandle, on the south-east by rolling Buena Vista Park, and on the west by huge and welcoming Golden Gate Park, invited the gamboling and frolic of nature's children. The weather was benign, the neighbors tolerant, the topography gentle, the ecology nurturant—and all combined to feed the cauldron of ideas and moods that characterized the flowering of hippiedom.

The currents of ideology and temper that served to generate a context for the hippie are quite difficult to characterize; they must be found within the social and political history of the time. In the late fifties and early sixties the huge student population across San Francisco Bay in Berkeley lay dormant. The most significant student events of those sedate Berkeley years were panty raids. Not so in San Francisco. The House Un-American Activities Committee, still propelled by ghosts of communist conspiracy, held hearings in San Francisco in 1960 during which hundreds of young protestors were literally washed down the steps of the City Hall in which the committee had convened. Later, in June of 1963, in defiance of a State Department travel ban, several of these same young people went to Cuba. They returned with a fragment of a political ideology and with an animosity against the established order; they also returned with an affection for olive drab uniforms and for beards.

Coincident with the civil rights activities taking place in the South, an Ad Hoc Committee to End Discrimination was formed in San Francisco. Its first target was a small chain of drive-in restaurants—Mel's—whose owner, Harold Dobbs, happened to be a candidate for mayor and who had the backing of the more conservative elements within the city. The sit-ins were thought to be effective; Dobbs was defeated. On the crest of this achievement a broad-based coalition of activist groups developed; a meeting held on November 5, 1963, brought together some 2500 people under the aegis of eight different organizations. Their common purpose was to end racial discrimination in San Francisco. Their first target was the San Francisco Hotel Association and their instrument, inspired by the civil rights experience of the South, was a sit-in at the Sheraton-Palace Hotel. The time was February to March, 1964. On this occasion, however, the struggle brought with it mass arrests and the allegation, if not the fact, of police brutality.

Thus, through a confluence of forces—through the events and experiences of the civil rights sit-ins in the South and the North, through the first rudimentary consciousness of a brutal war in Vietnam, through the hopes and the shattering disappointments of young people caught up in trying to change an implacable system, came the year 1964. It was a year of sit-ins, wade-ins, sleep-ins; a year of a presidential campaign that took on special local meaning when Barry Goldwater was nominated for the presidency by the Republican party meeting in the Cow Palace of San Francisco; a year of arrests at the local Cadillac Agency and the Bank of America; and a year of mass trials that ran for some six weeks and that affected well over one thousand people. In the summer of 1964 a group of seven hundred people were required to attend court from 10:00 A.M. to 4:00 P.M. each weekday. They had to stay in San Francisco and they had to live. What more reasonable way than to extend their solidarity into communal and cooperative arrangements and what more congenial place than the benign and accepting Haight-Ashbury?

The ideology, to the extent it could be captured, was a curious blend of the old "free spirit" coupled with a smattering of Marx, Mao, and Bakunin. Among other elements in the collage could be found Thoreau, Gandhi, Ho Chi Minh, Martin Luther King, Buddha, Lenin, Marcuse, Castro, Watts, Norman Brown, and—a little later—Timothy Leary and Bob Dylan. And then came the first rumblings from the other side of the bay—the sleeping giant of some 27,000 students had at last awakened. The Berkeley campus witnessed demonstrations directed against the *Oakland Tribune* for its bad civil rights record. Finally, provoked by campus policy constraining anti-Goldwater campaigning, there came the Free Speech Movement during which a police car was "liberated" in the heart of the campus and over seven hundred people, led by Joan Baez, marched into Sproul Hall singing "We Shall Overcome." A few hours later, they were carried out to paddy wagons by bewildered police.

Everything seemed to converge at once: Bob Dylan with his anomic wail, a still innocent quartet of Beatles whose long hair was found to be most attractive and worthy of emulation, the San Francisco Mime Troupe with their extravagant irreverence, an escalating war in Vietnam that presented an immediate threat to draft-age young men. A new music emerged, with new rock groups with strange names: the Jefferson Airplane, the Quicksilver Messenger Service, the Fugs, the Lovin' Spoonful, Big Brother and the Holding Company. Their "concerts," sometimes ad hoc in nature, included dazzling light shows and an incredible array of electronic acoustical enhancements.

And then—in the mid-1960s—the already bubbling stew of excitement, desperation, and confusion was spiced with Lysergic Acid Di-ethylamide-25, or LSD. The "movement" fragmented: one segment became more intensely and militantly political, even if they did not eschew drugs; the other turned inward for a salvation that was personal.

Of all the ingredients that went into that pot of ideological and behavioral stew the most potent and the most offensive to those who might otherwise have remained dispassionate was drug usage. Psychedelic drugs became the heart and soul of the original Haight-Ashbury culture. They were not peripheral, as some first thought or hoped—some parenthetical appendage to a movement based on other postulates; they were central. They provided the fabric and texture of the movement; psychedelia was the embodiment of all that was supposed to happen. The use of marijuana and of methamphetamines had already become rather commonplace among the emerging hippies. LSD was a powerful new addition to the armamentarium of mind-altering substances. Initially, the use of these chemicals was perceived as instrumental; the end was self-realization, and a liberation from middle-class thinking. Indeed, drug use was in those early and heady days embedded in ritual. Lighting was subdued, incense burned, the music of the sitar droned in the background, and the wise and compassionate guru—experienced in the mysterious ways of the trip—was there to lead the initiate.

In the early days, LSD was legal and it was also pharmacologically impeccable; only after its designation as an illegal and dangerous drug did there appear the adulterated dosages that confused and made so unreliable what could be bought from the street vendors. There were many apologists for psychedelic drugs usage: the more enterprising of the young ideologues invoked the classicists—Coleridge, Huxley, Baudelaire—and then added the druggy accounts of the Indian medicine man, the peyote eaters and mescaline-intoxicated shamans of America's romanticized aborigines. Of the contemporaries, the most artic-ulate and the most extreme of the acid missionaries was Timothy Leary. In his better moments, he would fill an auditorium with hundreds of curious young people. He would appear on stage in a white, almost diaphanous cloth wrap, chant a few pacific mantras, and begin a long and mystical argument for drug use as a path to awareness and higher consciousness.

"Turn on, tune in, and drop out" became a formulation that took on substantive meaning; turning on was a rather precise phrase for what was touted as an electrifying experience. If the concept of "cellular awareness" had any validity at all, it *must* be electrifying. The consciousness of untold past millennia, of going back in time, back to primordial man, back even further to the origins of life in its basic, molecular nature, and still further back to the chaos of the "big bang"—such consciousness could be attained, youth were told, by means of calculated dosages of lysergic acid. The Ranters, handicapped by scientific ignorance, could do no better in their day than to imagine a primordial Eden; thanks to drugs, the hippies were able to deal with all magnitudes of phenomena from DNA to galaxies. Some visions, nonetheless, were hardly distinguishable from the mystical ex-perience of Cromwellian times:

> I had a beatific vision on acid and I saw God as all the things people believe him to be, as the best as well as the worst. He is, as a person, all the personalities as he is conceived of by different religions at the same time. From his body there ra-diates tremendous emotion and some people think of him as love, because the love he radiates is so dazzling you cannot see him. Also, he is the person who knows the answers to all the secrets, to all the mysteries. He has the greatest mystic powers. He can do anything. He is fantastically awe-inspiring.[17]

The following accounts are more in keeping with the twen-tieth-century version of antinomianism as self-realization:

Acid and mescaline propelled me a little faster in the direction
I was going, opening up a whole world, the inner world. . . .
I experienced the tremendous creative power in the mind and
how when used properly it can change the whole world. It can
very certainly change oneself. The sense that the mind can be
the master of all things.

And:

Another major turning point was my experience in the commune, while I was on speed [methedrine] which made me reject
my priests' role. After a two-hour argument with one of the
girls in the commune, I saw what I was saying . . . saw that
she was right, that all the time we were playing the same game.
My ego sort of shattered and dissolved. I got into weird vi-
sionary things—semi-consciousness. I saw her as a sister and
all as brothers, all with one father. . . . I shouldn't be preaching to them, but listening to them. Then I realized that I should
be listening to myself. I got out of the game I was playing and
that left a void because it stripped me of a role.

If Timothy Leary was the great theoretician of psychedelic
drug use, Ken Kesey was its field manager. Kesey and his "Merry
Pranksters" toured the San Francisco Bay Area in Kesey's out-
rageously painted bus, with a retinue of winning young girls,
dispensing acid by the bucketful. At meetings and rallies, at im-
promptu and ad hoc gatherings, at parties and at rock concerts
he would openly and, at times, surreptitiously drop the chemical
into punch, cola, and ice cream. To confound things, the pranksters issued an open invitation for *all* to partake of the "acid test,"
including the soon-to-be stunned and stoned Hell's Angels. The
incongruity of flower-bedecked innocents consorting with burly,
tattooed bikers in a frenzy of hallucination bewildered the growing numbers of onlookers who had enough difficulty coping with
either of these groups alone. But it was the nature of the evolving
ethos that everybody was welcome to the new vision. "Turning
on," remember, was *good,* not necessarily in itself but as a means
to the end of insight and emancipation from the constraints of
bourgeois mentality. Only later did the use of drugs, now much
expanded in repertoire, become an end in itself—something to
be indulged in for "kicks."

The alliance of hippies with Hell's Angels did not last; in October 1965 the motorcycle club joined the Oakland police in blocking a march to the Oakland Induction Center.[18] Psychedelic drugs, evidently, were not enough to convert everyone to the new vision of peace on earth.

Hippie drug usage was coupled with sexual behavior that shocked and bewildered the larger community. It is difficult today to determine which of these two articles of hippie faith disturbed the good citizens of America more deeply. The hippies emerged just at the beginning of a larger sexual revolution that would deal a death blow to Puritan constraint and liberate American women. Many young women and girls, as did the men and boys, seized the opportunity to explore all kinds of sexuality; they painted their bodies; they *bared* their bodies; they made love, literally, not war; they used sexual terms in conversation that made their elders burn with indignation; and they did all this publicly and with a disdain for discretion. Indeed, the more shocking, the more authentic. When Lenore Kandel published her *Love Book,* a paean to eroticism, it was confiscated as an obscenity by the police. But sex was not dirty, as the Ranters had well known: it was divine.

Unfortunately, the new sexual freedom also provided an opportunity for the exploitation of nervous and uncertain young women by their male counterparts who could charge the unwilling with the heinous crime of being "hung-up." The range of verbalized attitudes in respect to the sexual ethic was wide:[19]

> It's [speaking of the institution of marriage] only a piece of paper, another one of the destructive forces if you take it seriously. Myself, I'm legally married. It was like an urge on New Year's Eve. I figured I'm hitching and if I'm stopped by the cops it would be better to be married than with a runaway chick. I see any two people living together as married. If they want to leave, O.K.—there should be nothing to prevent each from doing what they want to do."

And again:

> My ideal view of marriage is a communal life with a number of groups where within each group there exists a communal marriage with all adults and children. There are common fa-

thers and mothers, with transferring from group to group being possible for each individual. There is no binding by law or means other than love and the desire for the people to be there.

But some reports reveal occasional notes of cynicism: "I have gone through homosexual and heterosexual experiences and realize that nobody cared about me because they were just into physical fucking."

The apogee of hippiedom and of the flower child was the great festival held on January 14, 1967, in Golden Gate Park— a huge human "be-in" and gathering of the tribes attended by some ten to fifty thousand souls. The numbers vary with the estimator: conservative, disapproving police observers offer a low number, while spokesmen for the movement offer an enthusiastically extravagant number. In any event, the precise count is irrelevant; it was a large crowd and the phenomenon was of social and psychological significance. The date was chosen as most propitious by an astrologer who had once managed the Quicksilver Messenger Service and who was touted by the *Oracle*, the communities' new psychedelic newspaper. Allen Ginsberg, on that early morning, circumambulated the Polo Field while chanting a mandala of purification. The day, although starting with some menace, turned into one of beautiful sunshine.

The scene that greeted new arrivals as they crested the last rise and looked down on the sunken field was mind-boggling. A seemingly endless sea of people, tens of thousands. And all were present for a purpose too important for words, though a steady stream of words issued from the speakers' platform, at the east end of the field. The Diggers had set up tables to pass out thousands of turkey sandwiches, made from several dozen turkeys donated by Owsley Stanley [the meticulous student chemist who ground out impeccable LSD and who was reputed to have made a small fortune from the endeavor]. Owsley had also donated a lot of his latest LSD, White Lightning, and people were walking around in the crowd handing out these tiny white tablets, the most professional-looking and also the strongest LSD tablets yet.

As at the Love Pageant Rally and the New Years Wail, there were banners: some showing marijuana leaves, some in paisley patterns or solid colors. A number of people wore robes and exotic clothing. . . . many people brought fruit, flowers, incense, cymbals and tambourines, suitable for a genuine *mela*. Many had brought bells, mirrors, feathers or bits of fur, the kind of thing people had long carried around on Haight Street to blow the mind of a passing tripper.[20]

Allen Ginsberg led a chant, Timothy Leary recited his formula of "Turn on, tune in, drop out," Lenore Kandel read from her *Love Book*. The Jefferson Airplane was there, and so were the Quicksilver Messenger Service, the Grateful Dead, the Loading Zone, and other groups.

The event was scheduled to run from one to five. As the sun began to set, Gary Snyder blew on a conch shell, the ritual instrument of the Yamabushi sect of Japanese Buddhism, which he joined to the surprise of those who had expected him to become a Zen monk. Then Allen Ginsberg led a chant of "Om Shri Maitreya" to the Coming Buddha of Love. The crowd began to drift off. A number stayed, though, and under Ginsberg's leadership cleaned up the afternoon's accumulation of trash. Afterward they accompanied Ginsberg to the western edge of the park, about a mile away, and straggled across the highway to the Ocean Beach strand, where they built fires and chanted and prayed.[21]

It was a glorious event—a stupefying extravaganza of drugs and hope and silliness and innocence. It was also the death knell of the phenomenon.

For months national attention had converged on the events of the Haight-Ashbury. Indeed, the area attracted *international* attention. The newspapers, the magazines, and the national television networks found in the events of San Francisco a rich mine of reportable stories to fascinate and even charm voyeuristic readers and viewers.[22] The great human be-in provided the opportunity for further extravagance in media coverage. The apotheosis of attention was reached when the tourist buses began to ply the streets of the Haight:

On April 5 the Gray Line Bus Company did what the Gossiping Guru had predicted in the *Oracle*. It instituted a "San Francisco Haight-Ashbury District 'Hippie Hop' Tour," which it advertised as "the only foreign tour within the continental limits of the United States." Monday through Friday a Gray Line bus piloted by a driver "especially trained in the sociological significance" of the Haight would make a two hour expedition to the "Hashberry." Explorers were given a "Glossary of Hippie Terms."[23]

On June 8, one of the tour buses was commandeered by a Digger who handed out avocados and jubilantly announced that they had all been freed.

The publicity given the hippie movement, initially surprisingly sympathetic, made for a magnetic attraction. Each day brought an increment of new young people into the Haight-Ashbury seeking the freedom, the joy, the excitement, the girls, and the drug experience. They were not necessarily the same kinds of young people who had started it all. Already there were rumblings, by the more sober gurus, that all was not well. "Bad trips" were reported more and more frequently; alarming stories of the hazards of LSD appeared; and in October 1966 it was declared an illegal drug by the state of California. Ken Kesey was running from the law, and Timothy Leary also had his legal troubles. The Diggers, an offshoot of the San Francisco Mime Troupe, had to dispense free food, free clothes, and free everything to the needy as well as the not-so-needy; a free medical clinic was started to tend to the cut feet, respiratory infections, hepatitis, venereal disease, broken bones, and broken minds of new waves of young people. The skepticism as to what was happening is best described by a contributor to one of several local street publications:

> Pretty little sixteen-year-old middle class chick comes to the Haight to see what it's all about & gets picked up by a seventeen-year-old street dealer who spends all day shooting her full of speed again & again, then feeds her 3000 mikes [of L.S.D.] & raffles off her temporarily unemployed body for the biggest Haight Street gang bang since the night before last. The politics & ethics of ecstasy.
>
> Rape is as common as bullshit on Haight Street.[24]

Most people were not yet prepared to see it quite that way and a forthcoming "Summer of Love" was excitedly awaited as the greatest thing to happen, ever.

The eager anticipation was not shared by the city fathers. Predictions as to the numbers of people who might descend upon the Haight-Ashbury in the summer of 1967 were terrifying: Bill Graham, impresario of rock concerts, thought, perhaps hopefully, that the sum might amount to several millions; even the most conservative estimates were always in the tens of thousands. John F. Shelly, the mayor, wrote to the Board of Supervisors:

> I wish to emphasize at this time I am strongly opposed to any encouragement of a summer influx of indigent young people who are apparently being led to believe by a certain element of society their vagrant presence will be tolerated in this city. . . .
>
> I believe the Board of Supervisors should go on record as declaring as its policies that such migration is unwelcome; that existing ordinances be strictly enforced and that such migratory persons cannot be permitted to sleep in public parks or otherwise violate laws involving public health and the general peace and well-being of this community.
>
> Information should be widely promulgated that the City of San Francisco cannot provide food or shelter for such persons and that their presence here without adequate prior planning on their part for their necessities can only result in a chaotic condition detrimental to themselves and to the residents of San Francisco.[25]

In April the chief of police announced a series of orders to clean out the parks: no tents after 10:00 P.M. and no musical instruments after 9:00 P.M. The mayor's concerns were coincident with the activity of the Department of Health, provoked by wild speculation as to a forthcoming outbreak of bubonic plague, as it carried out inspections of some 1400 buildings within the Haight in the hopes of uncovering code violations. The crash pads turned out to be relatively normal and the department rather ruefully ceased its harassment.[26] HANC interjected a note of wisdom: "Haight-Ashbury is a state of mind as well as a geographic area."[27]

Maybe so, but there *was* a real problem. Thousands of young people, many of them still children, did in fact flock to the area that spring and summer and for many months thereafter. Converts had been won by the great gathering of the tribes; but very few were equipped with the mystique of loving peace. They came from all kinds of social backgrounds and with all the personal torment that can be found in any large population of people.

Many arrived penniless after hitchhiking from locations scattered across the country. The interstate highway had replaced the railroads as the means of transportation for this new army of antinomian vagrants. The on-and-off ramps of freeways throughout the area were always occupied by young people coming from or going to someplace. Some had the foresight to spell out, on readable placards, their intended destinations. Hitchhiking became ubiquitous throughout the nation; it was not perceived then, as it is now, as a source of danger, but the appearance even then belied the reality. Hitching a ride in the late 1960s *was* risky. But no matter how they arrived—most by thumb or by bus, some by plane, and a very few, still, riding the rods— they quickly found themselves in need. Some of the new arrivals were very young; many were official runaways. Where were they to sleep? And how to eat?

A crash pad was a place to rest one's weary bones; it may not have been invented in the Haight but it surely reached a high degree of refinement and institutionalization there. The ethic was one of sharing: space, food, drugs, or bodies. It was an ethic that was lived; crashing was the acceptable and expected device for securing shelter. Even the most raving and troubled people could usually find acceptance at one of the innumerable apartments or houses occupied by assorted people. Almost nobody, it seemed, lived with blood relatives; the new arrival lived, at first, with strangers. Later, perhaps, he or she would live with friends in some sort of loose or not-so-loose common arrangement.[28]

The urban commune was a more structured arrangement. Members usually had assigned responsibilities and obligations; many members were rather ordinary wage earners. Some of the communes were designed as conscious and calculated experiments in new family forms and sexual arrangements; some were organized around the drug experience; and some had a religious orientation, usually variants of Eastern theologies. Most communes invariably had a political structure, if only in the sense that living in a group inevitably leads to questions about who makes what decisions. Some communes were much more overtly political. Indeed, some communes were defined by the politics of their members. There were communes created by Venceremos veterans, and—much later—the revolutionary communes of Weathermen and even of such "organizations" as the Symbionese Liberation Army.

The commune was not necessarily a city phenomenon, however. In fact, the exodus to rural environments followed quickly upon the heels of the summer of love. It was time, some thought, to get out of what was rapidly becoming a nightmare and get on with the business of forging a new world. Well, at least a new community. A precedent already existed in the Morningstar Ranch, thirty acres of land in Sonoma County owned by Lou Gottlieb, a former Haight-Ashbury resident. The ranch had acquired a considerable reputation as a bucolic site for festivals of hallucinatories. But Morningstar was very loose, that is to say, hang-loose. It was more like an ordinary place to crash. The crash pad was marvelously informal.

Food was, likewise, there for the taking. The Diggers, for example, would distribute flyers:

> FREE FOOD   GOOD HOT STEW
> RIPE TOMATOES   FRESH FRUIT
> BRING A BOWL AND SPOON TO
> THE PANHANDLE AT ASHBURY STREET
> 4 PM   4 PM   4 PM   4 PM
> FREE FOOD   *EVERYDAY*   FREE FOOD
> IT'S FREE BECAUSE IT'S YOURS!
>
> the diggers[29]

And it *was* free and given without any expectation of gratitude. The Diggers, after all, had recently celebrated the Death of Money with a parade that drew 1000 people to Haight Street. But the demise of currency was not apparent to many; panhandling and dope dealing continued to be the predominant means of financial solvency.

The hippies may very well have added a novel dimension to the ancient craft of begging. In the past, the posture of the supplicant had been one of deference and self-denigration. The dramaturgy of the encounter between the parties consisted of a straightforward statement of inequality: "Poor, unfortunate me, unworthy as I am, helpless and stricken by misfortune—give me alms, worthy one; God or fortune or your own virtue has made you my better!" The act of begging was an exchange; in return for the handout might come a blessing, an expression of gratitude, a grovel, a trifle of material goods, or a horror show of mutilation and disease. The philanthropist could leave the encounter with the comfortable knowledge that he had gotten something for his beneficence; gratitude at the very least and the certainty that he had accumulated a credit for the inevitable term in purgatory. If the transaction aborted either because the terms seemed inequitable or uncalled for, there might be a growl or a mutter of complaint—even a flash of anger—but there was always *something* to remind the prospective donor that he was in a superior status.

The hippie turned the whole affair upside down. He or she solicited without self-abnegation. There was no groveling, no self-pity, no hint of despair. "Any spare change?" was accompanied by a smile, Mona Lisa–like in its inscrutable wisdom, and a demeanor that conveyed a sense of wholeness and good fortune. There was more than a hint that the transaction was not between equals; indeed, the smiling young person *condescended* to initiate the drama. The hippie, after all, could claim a superior moral stance—clearly evident in the liturgy of disengagement: "Have a nice day!" And this benediction was conferred whether or not the beggar had received his or her gift of alms. For the stunned passerby, confronted by a flower-bedecked and winsome young man or woman deigning to ask for "spare change," the experience could be most unsettling.

The theater of panhandling notwithstanding, the young people of the Haight had to survive. The "Have a nice day!" was not always heartfelt. Panhandling was a needed and common supplement to a meager subsistence derived from a variety of sources: the sharing that was endemic to the community at that time and typified by the activities of the Diggers; local merchants; public welfare officials when they were so inclined and could find some semblance of an appropriate categorical program; established private social agencies that, after an initial period of befuddlement, realized the existence of a real problem; ad hoc agencies that began to proliferate in rather novel forms; sometimes, monies from home; on occasion, work; and small-time drug dealing.[30]

This latter activity was pervasive and recognized as a legitimate source of petty cash as well as of drugs for personal use. Needless to say, it was not so perceived by the authorities. Arrests for the possession and dealing of drugs increased markedly and contributed to what amounted to a communitywide paranoia.[31] The narc was believed to lurk around every street corner. For the most part, drug dealing at that time was on a petty scale, consisting of small purchases and even smaller sales of marijuana, LSD, and amphetamines. Like much else in the community, the drug transaction was ritualized; buyer and seller would consummate the deal by sampling the substance in a rite of good fellowship and mutual trust. The typical unit of transaction for marijuana was the "lid," a quantity that hovered around one ounce. The kilo was, already, a sales unit for rather big-time operators. In 1967, the street price was something on the order of twelve dollars a lid. Much of a single purchase would be set aside for the vendor's own personal use and a good part of the rest would be given away. Dealing in drugs was *not* primarily to make money; it was to maintain for oneself a supply of the various substances.

This rather benign economy of drugs rapidly turned quite ugly. As the area became well known as a source of drugs to many kinds of people from outside the neighborhood, there was a growing influx of "strangers," who brought with them values and behaviors quite different from those of the original inhabitants. Second, the Haight-Ashbury was on the periphery of one of the black ghettos of the city, the Fillmore. Quickly, the burgeoning drug economy began to fall into the hands of a group of people for whom drug usage had a completely different meaning and for whom the profits to be found in drug sales were transcendent. Third, the kinds of drugs used by the inhabitants of the community underwent a transformation; the old standbys were still available but often of very uncertain quality. Owsley's perfect LSD was supplanted by all kinds of chemical intoxicants produced by fly-by-night operations, and some of these products could be fatal. Poorly manufactured or adulterated drugs became a major headache to the health and medical establishment; they also provoked the institution of various "hot-lines" to spread the word quickly about dangerous drugs on the streets. The streets were full of brand-new concoctions: STP, "hog," and many variants on "uppers" and "downers."

But the most telling new element that led to the wilting of the flower children was the mass of people who poured into the area lured by the promise of the summer of love. Mayor Shelly was correct: they came ill prepared and not knowing what they were getting into. Although the original hippies were clearly children of the middle classes, the new converts came from a more heterogeneous background.[32] Teenagers and preteens, running from their own homes for all kinds of reasons, found themselves in a disintegrating community. The elders of the Haight-Ashbury, perhaps in recognition of the monster that they had created, left for the hinterlands and the rural, communal expression of ideology and practice. They hoped for a formal closing of the era whose obituary was to be announced in revered ritual; a "Death of the Hippie" procession was held on October 6, 1967.

> The funeral procession began atop Buena Vista Hill at sunrise on Friday. "Taps" was played, candles were held aloft. Hippie and media emblems were consigned to a fire: copies of daily newspapers and the *Barb*, beads, reputed marijuana. Some eighty people took part in a procession down Haight Street, which was adorned for the day with a banner that read, "Death of Hippie Freebie, i.e., Birth of the Free Man." They bore a cardboard coffin with a representative hippie inside. After a "kneel-in" at the corner of Haight and Ashbury, the procession moved on to its destination, the Psychedelic Shop, where a record player was turned up loud to drown out the unscheduled screams of a girl bumming out on acid. The Psych Shop window was filled with signs: "Be Free." "Don't Mourn for Me, Organize." "Nebraska Needs You More."[33]

The summer of love had ended in an autumn of disintegration and death. The Gray Line canceled its tours; some rather chic boutiques boarded up their windows; the gay and outrageous costumes gave way to tatters and rags; the "spare change?" solicitation began to follow its old, timeless, and more orthodox scenario.

What was left was a small army of bewildered, hungry, and sick young people. The paroxysm of polymorphous drug use generated a substantial number of mentally troubled people—many of them had arrived in San Francisco with a history of psychological problems, but the hippie life often exacerbated whatever they came with.[34] The ambiance had become one of fear: predators were everywhere ready to steal, exploit, assault, and rape. The authorities, too, were out in force: narcotics agents to make arrests, police to apprehend runaways, draft evaders, AWOLs, and deserters.

The "original" hippie, if he or she could ever be separated from the nouveau, had already left. The hippies had been a group of bright young men and women who came from advantaged homes. They had renounced, if only for a while, the expectations of their parents and the bourgeois social ethos that had shaped their young lives, they had experimented with drugs, sex, and new life-styles, and then they had drifted back in varying degrees to a more conventional life.

One must take what they said quite seriously; they did not fit in with the world and hopes of their parents. It was a world that demanded glibness and social facility; it demanded a total commitment to rationality; and it demanded the acceptance of a constellation of values quite remote from immediate reality. The payoff for submission to these demands was "success," but the kind of success exemplified by their own parents' and neighbors' lives did not appeal to them—indeed, conventional measures of success appalled the hippie converts.

This line of argument has been put forward by many others,[35] but the hippies may well have been the first mass generation of disaffected people who had been raised in affluence. The world, from the vantage point of material possibility, was theirs. They had health, and baby-sitters, and orthodontia. And yet their internal life was chaos and loneliness.

How can this paradox be explained? The most obvious explanation is, in many ways, the most unappealing. Material advantage is not sufficient for personal coherence and direction. To put the argument in its most stark form: they were nurtured and nourished on a fraudulent promise and they perceived the sham. Having seen the sham, they found themselves in an impossible situation. It was no longer possible for them to continue on with their lives—working toward such orthodox objectives as higher education and a career—with the knowledge that such goals brought nothing but emptiness and superficiality. Success, in the tradition of their parents, was a most unpalatable accomplishment; they had the experience of their own eyes to tell them so. The transparent falsity of the promise could not be ignored. They took the only reasonable way out of this dilemma: they quit. They resigned from the middle class and its upwardly mobile tracks. They dropped out of conventional society and set off on a quest for new, better ways of living.

But most hippies could not continue their quests, and herein lies their tragedy. The price to be paid for dropping out was enormous. Turning one's back on conventional life usually led to poverty and all of the minor irritations and inconveniences that marginal subsistence entails. By withdrawing from conventional occupational pursuits and by separating themselves from their parents, hippies were faced with the *permanent* prospect of scrounging for their most elementary needs. Threadbare clothes, erratic diet, and homelessness were a *necessary* consequence of impoverishment. Once the "decision" to drop out was made, the poverty was no longer optional and the hippie, like marginally affiliated people at all times, was required to survive as best as he or she could. And this inevitably meant availing himself or herself of whatever welfare help obtainable, begging, petty theft, and whatever other forms of hustling he or she could devise.

Initially, such material impoverishment was not at all a burden; indeed, for some, it had a romantic appeal. But it is one thing to play at poverty and quite another to embrace it as a permanent feature of life. Marginal subsistence is, at best, uncomfortable, and only the most committed ideologues or those who have no alternative would be willing to endure it for very long. The amenities of affluence are powerfully seductive, especially when one is embedded in a society that makes such things so visible. The hippies, although they may have wished to, could not ignore or transform their larger social environment.

This inevitable and immutable fact brought to the hippie his or her most serious problem: harassment from the wider social system. A prime motivation for the people of the Haight was to be rid of what was seen as incessant *demand*. For the hippie, so long perplexed by incessant expectation, to search for and, indeed, create a "no hassle" world was paramount. Paradoxically, hippie culture, premised on the idea that one was *to be left alone*, brought down upon its members a veritable avalanche of hassle. Hippies were nagged, most persistently by the disapproval of their parents. At times the disapproval was timid; well-meaning moth-

ers and fathers were not always prepared to definitely criticize a
way of life so antagonistic to their own. One must sympathize with
such parents who—with the best of intentions—had raised their
children in a liberal and permissive fashion and now discovered
themselves betrayed by that child-rearing ideology. These parents did *not* approve of drugs or of sexual license. Eventually
they communicated their disapproval to their hippie children,
and thereby added to their discomfort and burden of uncertainty.

Perhaps parental hassles could have been endured. But hassles from the community at large, most often carried out by agents
of law enforcement, were another matter. Hippie behavior, was,
in some important measure, illegal behavior. A hippie's vulnera-
bility to arrest and imprisonment was real, if perhaps slightly exaggerated. Drug usage was fraught with some danger; drug
dealing was even more perilous. The illegality of drugs was a
source of great anxiety for hippies; they may have been contemptuous of law enforcement agencies in this regard but they could
never ignore the ever present possibility of being busted.[36]

The draft and the prospect of serving in Vietnam was also
a hassle. Some of the male residents of the Haight were fugitives
from the Selective Service system; many of the remainder were
engaged in a chronic struggle for deferments of various kinds.
It was a struggle that could become all-consuming and extend,
in some cases, over several years. The stakes were high: to lose
meant the army, and possibly Vietnam—a war for which they
had no stomach.

Even within the protective culture of the Haight-Ashbury
there was no way to escape these harassments. The "no-hassle"
world that the hippies hoped to create turned out to be a su-
perhassle. Hippieness backfired; longed-for peace and tranquility was overwhelmed by the realities of American society.
The larger community turned on the hippies, and, through ways
both direct and indirect, waged a vendetta against the young
men and women of the Haight.

In short, to have remained a hippie would have required a
relentless struggle against the coercive forces of convention. Most
were unwilling or unable to maintain the battle. It was easier to
drift back to conventional society. And especially so if one had
the prerequisites for succeeding. The hippie movement failed
because it could not insulate its members from the demands of

society in general nor could it offer enough rewards to compensate for continued struggle against such demands.

For a while, new recruits could lose themselves in the novelty of outrageous rebellion. It was fun; indeed, it was *supposed* to be fun. The ethos of the Haight-Ashbury put a premium on fun. Haight-Ashbury had a topsy-turvy ideology that transformed liabilities into assets. And more and more people were arriving with liabilities of psychic structure. The categories of personal stigma and deprecation within the straight world were absent in hippie culture. There was, in the Haight-Ashbury, no schizophrenia, no ugliness, no ineptitude, no bizarreness, no immorality, and no failure. It was the most benign of settings for people, especially among the latecomers, who suffered from the stigma of not being able to make it.

It was a noble and miraculous experiment—a world in which liability became asset, ineptitude became talent, disorganization became creativity, and all that was previously unacceptable and stigmatized became proper and beautiful. The hippie ideology was premised on being *kind*. They wanted to love and be loved. Alas, it did not work.

But there were legacies. The very special forms of musical expression born in the Haight went on to dominate pop music. The casualness of dress, too, persisted for a long while. And, sadly, the implicit legitimization of drug use continued to plague new generations but now it was shorn of ritual and sanctified context. And the place of women in the fabric and soul of antinomian life was elevated to a status of real equality.

The phenomenon was not restricted, by any means, to the locale of San Francisco; it had become a national, indeed, a worldwide expression. The hippie, or what *seemed* to look like the hippie, could be found everywhere, even—perhaps especially—in the remote and exotic regions of the planet. He could be found in Kathmandu or Elath or Manzanillo as well as in Cleveland or Madison. And he was as likely as not to be someone other than American. Indeed, *mobility* may have been one of the more profound legacies of the hippie phenomenon: the incorporation into the ethos of youth culture of an ability to pick up and go places—all kinds of places—and not worry about where one would find shelter.

5

Street People:

Harbingers of a New Residuum?

I don't have a home
and I live there
all the time.[1]

T HE hippie phenomenon was short-lived, but the demise of
the hippie was not at all apparent to the public at large.[2]
The cities and roads of America continued to be full of young
people who had all the same features of dress, baggage, deco-
ration, language, and beliefs in the tenets of what had come to
be known as the "counterculture." The casual observer thought
that these new young homeless were the *same* people as the hippies. In time and as the differences became more obvious, the
new group of homeless youth became known as "street people"
or "road people."[3]

Street people first appeared on the periphery of the major
university campuses of the country and in the larger metropolitan cities. The street person was a phenomenon of Cambridge/
Boston, New York, Miami, and Ann Arbor; of Madison, Austin,
Boulder, Seattle, Portland, Vancouver; of San Francisco, Berkeley, Isla Vista, and Los Angeles. He and, increasingly, she could
be found trudging the streets with backpack and bedroll. The
males were usually bearded; both men and women dressed rather
shabbily but almost always with dabs of color and panache; both
sexes wore beads and bangles; some street people carried a mus-

ical instrument, typically, a guitar or a harmonica; and they were often accompanied by a dog or a cat—more rarely by a small child. They would ask the passerby for "spare change" and bless donors and nondonors alike with the benediction "Have a nice day." Some street people were *very* young.

The streets, by now, had become permanent fairs replete with jugglers, poets, mimes, musicians, and a host of artisans of varying talent who sold their wares in makeshift street shops:

> [The street vendor] is completely involved in selling his wares with the full regalia of the street market around him. He is part of the mad melange of hippie street costume—Greek-sandaled, feet peeking beneath harem pantaloons encased in a fringed American Indian suede jacket, topped with a beaded head band on the forehead or the long hair and bare feet locked between a flour sack with stars, buttons, and bells, decorations that bedecked individuals for other functions in the past and present of this nation. He displays items that have some appeal to both hip and "straight" walkers of the public pavements, and he transacts his sales on a cash and carry basis, the exceptions to this being more rare than regular. He lodges himself adjacent to another peddler, and as a body, they ordinarily span a three or four block area in front of the city's oft-frequented shops and stores.[4]

The articles for sale might include hashish pipes of polished rock, organic oatmeal cookies, pretty pebbles, shells, driftwood, tie-dyed shirts, beaded headbands, earrings, knitted bras (even in a braless era), photographs of god knows what, or the ubiquitous candles.

The ambiance of the locale has been described by Jerry Rubin:

> Thousands of refugees of New York and the Midwest flocked to live on the streets of Berkeley. It was an easy life. The weather was warm and the seasons hardly changed, so you didn't need to buy winter clothing. You could always get by selling dope. Or you could hawk the *Barb* on the weekend and make enough money for the rest of the week. There were always guilty professors to panhandle. And some people started handicraft industries—sold jewelry, candles and other things they made—right on the Avenue. Nobody starved on the streets of Berkeley.

A whole new culture burst forth outside the biggest university in the history of the world. Telegraph Avenue was five blocks long and lined with bookstores, outdoor cafes, poster shops and underground movie theaters. Dig the straight student who came out of a Los Angeles suburb to get an education at Berkeley. Heading for his dormitory or apartment after a hard day at school, he passed down Telegraph Avenue: like walking through the revolution on the way home.[5]

Rubin was wrong on several counts: the life, as we shall see, was *not* easy; people may not have starved but they were frequently hungry; the "revolution" was more mirage than reality, although at the time it had every appearance of being more durable and it surely terrified the establishment; and the street vendors of the "penny economy" were struggling entrepreneurs in the grand tradition—most aspired to nothing more than to get off the sidewalk and into one of the *real* shops just a few feet away.[6]

The street person came to where he was and left to where he was going seemingly without purpose. In the tradition of the hippie, he hitched:

[The road leading to the on-ramp] is littered with the disheveled young, some with outstretched thumbs, others with signs in picturesque neo-graffiti, and all seeking access to Interstate 80 and the road. . . . The prime asset in the contest is an attractive girlfriend. The biggest handicap is a dog.[7]

This scene, perhaps with less commotion, could be found at many other sites across the country.

The existence of street people presented a serious problem to the civic authorities of the communities to which they gravitated. They were a matter for the police. In those days of large, public, out-of-doors political demonstrations and acts of civil disobedience, street people were easily swept up and into acts of disorder and sometimes violence. A blatant drug traffic always hovered around any presence of street people. More significantly, however, street people were often hungry, sick, frightened, and homeless. Conventional social agencies and medical services were overwhelmed by the variegated need presented by the street person and not at all sure about how to respond to needs of so untraditional a clientele. Eventually, new social and health services, most predicated on the notions of self-help and consumer participation, arose to attend to the needs of the street population.[8]

Many of these organizations, plagued by uncertainty as to whom exactly they were serving, did attempt to keep simple statistics about their clientele, but they were severely hampered in this effort by the ethos of the population they served. Street people were disinclined to interact with bureaucratized services and record keepers—some because of serious problems with law enforcement agencies, some out of a distaste for any organizational form, and many out of a resentment of those they perceived to be powerful moral agents (social workers, physicians, and clergymen—among others). This pervasive desire for anonymity and secrecy made data gathering counterproductive to the rendering of the needed service. It was out of a pressing need for basic data to guide these established and ad hoc social services that in the spring of 1973 a study was conducted of the street people of Berkeley, California. Its intent was to provide a systematic descriptive portrait of a population of people who confronted the community with novel problems and service needs.

What follows is that portrait. Although the data obviously derive from a very specific sample of people, I have no reason to suppose that the more general population of young men and women—living on the streets throughout America—could have been very much different. In fact, most Berkeley street people had *come* from someplace else and most would *go* to someplace else eventually. For many people in the sample, it was merely an accident of time that found him or her in Berkeley during the week of the study survey.

The Berkeley Emergency Food Project was the survey site. Located in the heart of the area called South Campus, the Food Project was widely known to serve all comers for free, without the missionary zeal of the more traditional soup kitchens that still existed in the old skid-row areas of Oakland and San Francisco. The Food Project's "eligibility criteria" did not exclude *anybody*. The life circumstances of the prospective subjects seemed to compel most of them to eat there at least once in a while.

Thus, we reasoned that the Food Project's clients would offer a good cross-section of street people.

There was a great amount of seasonal variation in the street population. The goal was to describe those who were not merely summer "tourists" taking advantage of a free meal to save on travel costs. Thus, data were collected during the "off season." During the week of March 26–31, 1973, a detailed census was taken of every person who was fed at the Food Project. Further, a subsample of these patrons was selected for in-depth interviews. In all, some 1105 meals were served during that week to 452 different people. Of these, 295 were included in the final sample. In the statistical portrait that follows, the totals do not always sum to that number because not all subjects were willing to respond to every question.

Demographic Characteristics: Age, Race, and Sex

Of the 295 respondents in the study population, 239 (81 percent) were males and 56 (19 percent) were females. The percentage of women in this census was unusually high compared with previous populations of transient or homeless people that had been systematically studied; the percentage clearly reflects one of the more dubious rewards of the emerging emancipation of women.

Respondents' ages ranged from fifteen to sixty-two, with a median age of 22.7, and a mean age of 23.6. Table 5–1 gives more detail about the age distribution of subjects by sex. As table 5–1 indicates, the population was young: nearly three-quarters were aged twenty-five or less. Women, 62.5 percent of whom were under twenty-one, were considerably younger than the men. In fact, nearly one-fourth of the women would have been considered juveniles under the laws of California. Further, of those respondents between eighteen and twenty-five years of age, one-fifth (19 percent) had originally left their home while still juveniles; many, of course, were runaways. Women who had left home while under age eighteen years were greatly overrepresented in the "older" group of eighteen- to twenty-five-year-olds.

Table 5–1
Age by Sex

	Male (N = 238)	Female (N = 56)	Total (N = 294)
Under 18	2.5%	23.2%	6.5%
18–20	16.4	39.3	20.8
21–25	49.6	30.4	45.9
26–30	23.1	5.4	19.7
31–35	5.0	1.8	4.4
36 or over	3.4	0.0	2.7
Total	100.0	100.0	100.0

Table 5–2
Age by Race and Sex

	Black Males (N = 33)	White Males (N = 192)	White Females (N = 50)	All* (N = 292)
Under 18	0.0%	3.1%	20.0%	6.5%
18–20	12.1	17.2	44.0	20.8
21–25	60.6	46.9	28.0	45.9
26–30	21.2	23.4	6.0	19.7
31–35	6.1	5.2	2.0	4.4
36 or over	0.0	4.2	0.0	2.7
Total	100.0	100.0	100.0	100.0

*Includes Asians, Indians, Chicanos, and Latinos, and one black woman.

Most of the street population (82.9 percent) was white. Blacks comprised 11.6 percent, Hispanics 2.1 percent, American Indians 2.1 percent, and Asians 1.4 percent. The small Hispanic group was composed mostly of Puerto Ricans; of the four Asians surveyed, two were Filipino, one was Chinese, and one Japanese.

The black subjects were, with one exception, male, and tended to be somewhat older than their white male counterparts, and considerably older than white women.

Education

The sample population was not well educated. In fact, they had not achieved a level of education equal, for their age cohort, to the population at large. Nationwide in 1972 only some 18 percent of people between the ages of twenty and twenty-four had *not* completed high school.[9] Even allowing for the youth of those in the study sample, their educational attainment was not then, and probably never would be, equal to the population at large. Of those street people twenty-five years old or younger, 36.7 percent had not completed the twelfth grade.

In respect to all respondents, nearly one-third (32.5 percent) had not graduated from high school. Another 27 percent had graduated from high school, but had never entered college. Of the 40 percent who had enrolled in college, 62.3 percent dropped out before completing any degree. Only 9.2 percent of respondents had graduated from a four-year college.

. Among street people, women and black men then were less educated than white men. The women included only two graduates of a four-year college; almost 43 percent of the women in the sample never finished high school. Of the black men, 46.6 percent had failed to finish high school, and only one individual had graduated from college. Table 5–3 displays the educational achievement of respondents by race and sex. Many (43 percent) of the respondents said they hoped to return to school, and quite

Table 5–3
Educational Achievement by Race and Sex

	Black Males (N = 30)	White Males (N = 186)	White Females (N = 49)	All (N = 283)
Less than 9th grade	13.3%	5.4%	6.1%	7.4%
9th, but less than 12th grade	33.3	22.6	36.7	25.1
High school graduate	20.0	24.7	34.7	27.2
Partial college	30.0	35.5	18.4	31.1
College graduate or more	3.3	11.8	4.1	9.2
Total	100.0	100.0	100.0	100.0

a few others (27 percent) were unsure. From the interview data, however, it was clear that those who wished to return to school had already achieved the most—both with regard to grade level and prior academic success while still in school. Of those indicating some desire to return to school, more than one-half (52.2 percent) cited lack of money, housing, or child care as the major obstacle.

Geographic Origins

The street people of Berkeley, referring to their place of birth and childhood upbringing, came from almost every state in the nation. In addition, some 2.5 percent were originally from Canada, 4.2 percent from Western Europe, and 2.4 percent from other countries spread across the globe. Only 8.7 percent of the subjects were natives of the San Francisco Bay Area, although 18.1 percent had been born in California. The largest number of respondents (26.7 percent) came from the Middle Atlantic region—specifically the states of New York, New Jersey, and Pennsylvania. Second only to California as the geographic source of most street people were the East Central states, which contributed 11.1 percent of the population. The street people came primarily from city backgrounds, particularly the urbanized, industrial areas of the country. Some 55.3 percent were from the huge metropolitan areas: New York City, Philadelphia, Chicago, Los Angeles. Only 22.2 percent came from cities of between 10,000 and 100,000 inhabitants which were not located near (within fifty miles of) a large urban area. A mere sixteen individuals (5.6 percent) came from rural America: those towns with a population under 10,000 not situated near a large city.[10]

Residence in Berkeley

The street people were highly mobile but, as will be seen, included some stable elements within the population. In the discussion that follows, the word "residence" must not be taken too literally; it usually denotes the place where respondents were crashing during the time they had been in town. While table 5–4 shows that nearly one-third had been in Berkeley only one month or less, and almost 60 percent for less than six months, approximately one-fourth had been around for over a year. As a group, blacks had the longest "residential" tenure. The sample revealed a group—10.6 percent of the total population—consisting of people who had a "stable" residence outside of Berkeley, usually in Oakland, Richmond, or San Francisco. These were individuals who had been drawn to Telegraph Avenue for what its social structure provided. Frequently, these "outside" street people were viewed, by both police and social workers, as predators who used the Telegraph area as their place of illicit business. They were characterized by such officials as gamblers, thieves, dealers, con men—in short, as the area's hustling population. The interview data, however, did not reveal that these "nonresidents" were any more involved in such activities than Berkeley's "own."

Thus far, we have seen that the street people of Berkeley, and probably those of many other communities, were a population composed primarily of young, white males who were not native to the area; who come from urban, and often Eastern parts of the country; who had been in the city a rather brief

Table 5–4
Length of Time in Berkeley by Race and Sex

	Black Males (N = 32)	White Males (N = 185)	White Females (N = 50)	All (N = 282)
week or less	6.3%	21.6%	20.0%	18.8%
days–1 month	3.1	13.0	22.0	13.1
weeks–6 months	21.9	23.2	30.0	25.2
months–1 year	12.5	5.1	6.0	5.2
3 mos–2½ yrs	25.1	12.4	8.0	13.5
More than 2½ yrs	9.4	11.4	6.0	10.6
Residence outside Berkeley	18.7	10.3	8.0	10.6
Total	100.0	100.0	100.0	100.0

period of time; and whose academic education had been short-lived. This simple portrait, though, masks the fact that there were subpopulations of blacks and women who had somewhat different demographic features, and who were—although numerically fewer—distinct elements of the population known then as street people.

Family Background

Apart from knowing the *places* these young people came from, it is of interest to note the kinds of families within which they were reared and nurtured. For the most part, these families had been at least superficially structurally intact. Thus, 61.6 percent of the respondents spent their childhood with both natural parents; the remaining 38.4 percent experienced varying degrees of family disruption, usually the divorce or separation of parents.

Among blacks, however, just the opposite situation obtained: 72 percent came from one-parent or otherwise structurally fragmented families. (See table 5–5.)

The mean number of children in the families of all respondents was 3.9. Blacks tended to come from larger families: the mean number of children in their families was 5.3. A substantial number of street people, 43.3 percent, were eldest children and 9.7 percent were only children. Men, far more frequently than women, were the eldest child. Only children were primarily white males. The women in the sample were, in most cases, middle children.

The parents of street people were typically born in urban environments. Thus, 71 percent of the fathers, and 67.5 percent

Table 5–5
Family Type by Race and Sex

	Black Males (N = 25)	White Males (N = 157)	White Females (N = 46)	All (N = 245)
Intact	28.0%	66.9%	69.6%	61.6%
Disrupted	72.0	33.1	30.4	35.4
Total	100.0	100.0	100.0	100.0

of the mothers were born in cities of 100,000 or more. Black parents, however, came frequently from small, rural towns (40.6 percent); they were, apparently, representative of the large migration of blacks from rural to urban areas that occurred during and after World War II.

Most street people came from residentially stable families. Of all respondents' families, 60.5 percent had lived in only one city prior to the time the subject left home. Only 9.1 percent of the families could be considered itinerant, as defined by a history of chronic movement from city to city.[11] Of these "nomadic" families, over half were military; 5 percent of the respondents were "army brats," the sons or daughters of career servicemen.

Significantly, the socioeconomic background of these subjects—though far from homogeneous—was quite different from that of most hippies of a decade earlier. The occupational status of subjects' fathers is given in table 5–6 and is based on a hierarchical ordering and elaboration of the occupational code of the United States Census. The ten categories were briefly defined

Table 5–6
Fathers' Socioeconomic Status by Race

		Black (N = 14)	White (N = 172)	All (N = 199)*
High	10	0.0%	7.0%	6.0%
	9	0.0	13.4	12.6
	8	0.0	7.6	7.0
	7	0.0	19.2	17.1
	6	14.3	8.1	8.5
	5	7.1	10.5	10.6
	4	0.0	6.4	6.5
	3	14.3	5.8	6.5
	2	42.9	15.6	20.1
Low	1	21.4	3.5	5.0
Total		100.0	100.0	100.0

*Because of ambiguous, and sometimes spiteful responses (e.g., "drunk"), the percentage of missing data on this variable was very high. For all subjects it was 32.5% (including 6.2% who never had a father); for whites, 29.2%; for blacks, 57.6%. For what seemed to be emotional reasons, some respondents simply skipped the survey section on family background—even when they completed all other parts. Most variables concerning family had roughly 20% missing data.

as follows: categories 1 and 2 include unskilled laborers and
service providers (e.g., cooks, porters); categories 3 and 4, the
semiskilled (bus drivers, some mechanics); categories 5 through
8, skilled laborers, craftsmen, technicians, and some professionals (typesetters, lithographers, bookkeepers, nurses, teachers, de-
signers); and categories 9 and 10 include the occupational elite:
doctors, lawyers, engineers, architects, etc. Table 5–6 is quite
telling: the street people of the mid-1970s were a downwardly
mobile population. The educational achievement of the fathers
was higher than that of the subjects. Some 34.2 percent of fathers
graduated from college as opposed to only 9.2 percent of the
subjects. In addition, while 25.6 percent of the fathers failed to
finish high school, 32.5 percent of respondents had failed to
finish. Even though street people were still young, and were
theoretically able to return to school, their circumstances suggest
that return would be unlikely. In fact, the phenomenon of educational slippage was one important indicator of the significant
downward mobility that appeared to characterize street people
as a population.

It should be noted, further, that not only were the fathers,
on the whole, better educated than their children, but that mothers too had obtained a higher educational level, though not by
so wide a margin. In spite of the downward mobility of the street
people in respect to the educational attainment of their fathers,
there still existed a discernable and direct relationship between
fathers' and subjects' educational achievement for the white respondents. That is, subjects who did not finish high school tended
more frequently than better educated respondents to have fathers who did not finish high school. Similarly, street people who
had at least begun college were more likely to have fathers who
had reached that level. Table 5–7 illustrates this relationship
between the educational attainment of white respondents and
that of their fathers.

Finally, in respect to the familial background of the Berkeley
street people, they were not reared in homes with strong religious
sentiments; their parents' religious behaviors were, by and large,
nominal ones. Thus, as measured by the frequency of church
attendance, fathers attended church hardly at all, and mothers
only slightly more often. Blacks tended to come from more re-

Table 5–7
Educational Achievement of Whites: Father by Subject

| | | Fathers' Level | | |
	Less than 12th	High School	At Least Some College	*Total*
Less than 12th (N = 47)	29.8	23.4	46.8	100%
High School (N = 49)	15.4	22.4	59.2	100%
At Least Some College (N = 84)	17.9	21.4	60.7	100%

Subjects' Level

Table 5–8
Subjects' Childhood Religious Affiliation by Race and Sex

	Black Males (N = 28)	*White Males (N = 167)*	*White Females (N = 46)*	*All (N = 255)*
Protestant	64.3%	37.8%	44.7%	42.0%
Catholic	21.4	37.8	29.8	34.9
Jewish	0.0	9.1	12.8	8.2
Others	0.0	1.2	0.0	1.2
None	14.3	14.0	12.8	13.7
Total	100.0	100.0	100.0	100.0

ligious families than whites; 57.7 percent of black mothers attended church regularly, and 55.6 percent of black respondents attended regularly as children. Among whites only 34.3 percent went to church often while growing up, but white females were more apt to be regular attenders than white men (47.8 percent and 30.5 percent, respectively). Table 5–8 shows the religions in which respondents were raised. In terms of their own and current religious sentiments, only 11 percent responded with a conventional preference (Catholic, Protestant, or Jewish); 64.2 percent indicated "none" (a specific category choice); and 24.8 percent indicated one of the more exotic or cultish sects. Most of the latter were of Eastern bent, but of these sixty-three individuals, eleven (17.5 percent) identified themselves as "Jesus

Freaks." Those who claimed to be devotees of Eastern religions were predominantly white.

To sum up this portrait of the family backgrounds of the street people, they came from essentially intact and stable urban and suburban families. Their fathers, for the most part, were employed in blue-collar and less prestigious white-collar occupations; only 18.6 percent of the subjects came from the upper reaches of the middle class. The parents of the respondents were much better educated than their children; and the parents also had more conventional religious and political convictions. In short, street people came from families that, on the surface at least, were rather ordinary. It would seem a reasonable assumption that their parents were typical American folk: upward aspiring, hardworking, and hoping that their children would achieve some economic affluence and live a rather conventional and respectable life. It was not to be so.

Life on the Streets

The study subjects were hungry people. Their hunger was, of course, at least a partial artifact of where we found them. However, the most compelling observation that emerged from the data was that the hunger of street people was a consequence of what can only be construed as an authentic poverty. A resounding 86.7 percent were unemployed. The remaining 13.3 percent were engaged in the most marginal and erratic types of work—often on a temporary and part-time basis. In the absence of conventional employment, the street person engaged in various income-generating activities or relationships. Table 5–9 presents the subjects' sources of income by race and sex. Table 5–10 gives the total income received by respondents from these various sources during the month prior to the census. If tables 5–9 and 5–10 are viewed together, some interesting patterns emerge. First, with reference to sources of income (table 5–9), we see that blacks and women tended to be the best utilizers of public assistance, but that the population as a whole, despite its obvious

Table 5-9
Sources of Income by Race and Sex[a]

	Black Males (N = 29)	White Males (N = 181)	White Females (N = 50)	All (N = 278)
Job	10.3%	14.9%	10.0%	13.3%
Savings	6.9	19.9	28.0	19.4
Unemploy. ins.	0.0	3.3	0.0	2.5
Welfare	31.0	13.3	20.0	15.8
Food stamps	6.9	7.2	12.0	7.9
Social Security	0.0	2.2	2.0	1.5
Parents, relatives	13.8	19.9	34.0	22.7
Spouse/sig othr[b]	10.3	6.1	26.0	10.4
Friends	41.4	32.0	30.0	33.1
Panhandling	37.9	39.0	55.0	41.9
Drug dealing	37.9	20.3	16.0	20.8
"Fencing"	13.8	1.7	0.0	2.9
Stealing	10.3	15.5	4.0	11.9

[a]The precise form of the question put to respondents was: "Please check any of the following sources you had obtained money from in the last month." The percentages total more than 100 because most subjects checked more than one source of income.
[b]Few street people (4.4%) were married, though more (16.7%) had been through unsuccessful marriage relationships.

Table 5-10
Total Income During the Past Month by Race and Sex

	Black Males (N = 28)	White Males (N = 155)	White Females (N = 44)	All (N = 243)
$0–50	28.6%	47.7%	45.5%	47.3%
$51–100	21.4	18.1	18.2	18.1
$101–150	21.4	7.1	6.8	8.2
$151–200	10.7	7.7	15.9	9.1
$201–250	3.6	8.4	6.5	7.0
$251 +	14.3	11.0	6.8	10.3
Total	100.0	100.0	100.0	100.0

impoverishment, did not draw much from the welfare dole. This situation can best be explained by considering the nature of direct assistance programs, and the eligibility requirements in existence at that time. Federal programs had stringent categorical limitations. Essentially, the only two federally funded programs available to this population were Aid to the Totally Disabled (ATD) and Aid to Families with Dependent Children (AFDC). ATD required that the recipient be totally disabled (i.e., unable to work in the foreseeable future) by some physical or psychological infirmity. The applicant needed to be able to prove the validity of his claim; in the case of those applying for a psychiatric disability, proof consisted of a psychiatric evaluation and, usually, submission of a verifiable history of mental hospitalization. The maximum grant at the time of the survey was approximately $180 per month. ATD generally took four to six months to obtain.

AFDC was typically available only to single women with children, but men with custody of their children were also eligible. It was relatively easy to get, and pregnant women could also receive benefits. AFDC grants varied depending on family size, but for families with one child the average grant was between $180 and $200 per month. AFDC benefits could start within a week of application.

Alameda County also had a General Assistance Program (GA). Maximum benefits were $100 per month, and recipients needed to be deemed "temporarily unable to work." Benefits could be obtained by "employables," but with imposing eligibility requirements and documentation. All public assistance programs, including the federal Food Stamps program, and California's Medi-Cal plan, had eligibility criteria that effectively excluded significant numbers of street people. First, an applicant needed two forms of acceptable identification, a requirement that presented serious problems for many street people. The theft of personal belongings always plagued the street person and many were either unaware of the procedure whereby identification could be replaced or they did not have the money to pay the fee to obtain a duplicate birth certificate. In addition, a surprisingly large number of street people—especially women—were unable to drive, and had never had a driver's license. Second, an applicant needed to have a current address—an obstacle of no small consequence for people who are *homeless.* Eligibility for food stamps required the recipient to have cooking facilities; a hot plate or makeshift apparatus in a residential hotel was not a sufficient facility.

This rough sketch of public assistance eligibility requirements for Alameda County, California—a county that had a relatively liberal program—explains in large measure the low utilization of welfare and food stamps by Berkeley street people. Blacks and women were more "fortunate."

With regard to women, 22.4 percent of white female respondents either had children with them or were pregnant. The "upper middle class" among street women, as indicated by table 5–9, was primarily composed of AFDC mothers. Blacks were better welfare utilizers for reasons that will become clearer when I discuss frequencies of mental hospitalization. To anticipate, blacks were more likely to have been hospitalized and were thus in a better position to be eligible for ATD.

In summary, table 5–9 indicates that among street people, white women most often had legitimate sources of income, and black males least often had legitimate sources, with the exception of welfare recipients. Women, typically younger and on their own for a shorter time, more often received some support from parents or relatives. On the whole, it appears that almost all street people were heavily reliant for money on friends, panhandling, and other forms of scrounging. As we see from table 5–10, nearly two-thirds of the population were surviving on $100 per month or less; and many of those who had more were the beneficiaries of some form of public aid.

If authenticity is the issue, then, the street people of the early 1970s surely qualify for the dubious distinction of living in real poverty. The threadbare squalor associated with the street person was not cultivated, and not self-imposed; bare feet and tattered clothes were, in most instances, the best that they could do for themselves.

As to their willingness to engage in employment, only thirty-four (16.5 percent) of the respondents did not want to work.[12] Some 77.3 percent had repeatedly sought work in the past year and were repeatedly rebuffed. Of those subjects who had sought work during the year prior to the survey, 35.6 percent had been turned down for every job for which they applied. About one-third of the respondents claimed that they would take *any* job that they were offered, and an additional 29 percent objected only to "bad conscience" jobs for which in all probability they were not qualified: positions in law enforcement, arms manufacture, and the like. The others had, for the most part, objections to what they thought might be particularly boring, poorly paid employment. Still, many of these individuals expressed a desire to work at nearly anything "interesting."

The self-reported skills and occupational histories of respondents left no doubt as to their employment marginality. When asked if they had a skill with which they could earn a living, 62.8 percent said they did; 11.2 percent were unsure, and 26 percent frankly admitted that they did not. As it turns out, however, most of those who reported the possession of a skill (78 percent) indicated that what they knew best to do was no more than, for example, to punch a cash register, trim hedges, or mold candles. The remainder claimed skills in the traditional crafts (plumbing, carpentry, etc.), but their proficiency in such tasks should be viewed skeptically.

Their occupational histories and employment patterns, such as they were, confirm the reality of a dearth of vocational skills and rather dismal prospects for anything more than very marginal employment. Fifty-seven percent of the subjects had a history of chronic unemployment; one-quarter of this perennially unemployed group had never worked. Many other subjects (19.1 percent) had been employed only sporadically, and of all respondents who had at some time been employed, 51.3 percent had worked only short-term or casual jobs, never being employed for longer than a few months at a time.

The long-term implications of such poor skills and erratic and meager occupational histories for a group of young people whose schooling (such as it was) was more likely at an end, is obvious and ominous. It portends a permanent membership in the ranks of the residuum.

Lack of employment and a consequent lack of income made survival on the streets and in transit a difficult task. Food and shelter were obtained cheaply and irregularly—wherever they could be found. The Berkeley Emergency Food Project was a regular source of sustenance for nearly half of the subjects, meaning that they ate there at least five nights a week. The proportion of such "regulars" at the Food Project was essentially equal across all racial and sexual groups. When street people did not eat at the Food Project they managed in the ways shown in table 5–11.

Restaurant-going was an important social activity for a group of people whose means did not permit luxuries. Sitting in a restaurant, sipping coffee, and talking with friends was cheap entertainment, as well as an excellent way to keep warm and dry. Also, there may have been some overlap between those who indicated that they "cook at home" and those who were fed by friends. By far, the majority of street people could best be described as crashers—they had found someone or some group to provide them with shelter and sometimes food for a night or two or three. In some of the more permanent crash settings this rent-free situation could extend over several weeks. "Cooking at home," then, could be synonymous with being cared for by friends or acquaintances.

Table 5–12 gives a more precise indication of how street people were sheltered. Table 5–12 can be somewhat misleading because it probably underestimates the number of "homeless" among this population. A better indicator of the prevalence of homelessness may be the percentage of individuals who pay no rent. Table 5–13 shows the amount of rent paid by respondents.

Table 5–11
Main Sources of Meals Other than the
Food Project
(N = 244)

Restaurants or markets	36.0%
Cooks at home	27.0
Friends	19.7
Don't eat	7.4
Steal food	6.6
Find food in garbage	3.3
Total	100.0

Table 5–12
Living Arrangements
(N = 292)

House	Apartment	Hotel	Crashing	Total
15.2	18.7	9.0	57.1	100.0%

Table 5–13
Rent Paid per Month by Race and Sex

	Black Males (N = 32)	White Males (N = 186)	White Females (N = 50)	All (N = 285)
None	50.0%	66.1%	70.0%	66.0%
$1–60	15.7	16.7	12.0	15.1
$61–80	15.6	15.1	8.0	13.3
$81 or more	15.6	2.2	10.0	5.6
Total	100.0	100.0	100.0	100.0

Patterns of Transience

In addition to looking at respondents' current living arrangements, information was gathered concerning their detailed itineraries extending from the time they had first left home. From these chronologies a crude typography can be constructed. The people in the sample tended to fit into three categories:

"Rooters"—Those who had lived primarily in one city since leaving home

"Nesters"—Those who had spent most of their time in only two or three cities; i.e., those who had settled into at least one city for six months or more at a time

"Chronics"—Those who had never spent an appreciable length of time in any one place, but who moved about— either in a discernible pattern, or seemingly at whim

Table 5–14 gives the frequency of these patterns by race and sex.

Table 5–14
Patterns of Transiency by Race and Sex

	Black Males (N = 27)	White Males (N = 156)	White Females (N = 46)	All (N = 243)
Rooters	15.5%	12.2%	15.2%	14.4%
Nesters	25.9	19.9	2.2	16.9
Chronics	55.6	67.9	82.6	68.7
Total	100.0	100.0	100.0	100.0

Table 5–15
Length of Time Away from Home by Race and Sex

	Black Males (N = 26)	White Males (N = 167)	White Females (N = 47)	All (N = 255)
6 months or less	7.7%	6.0%	36.2%	11.8%
7 months to 1 year	0.0	9.0	12.5	5.6
13 mos. to 2 yrs.	11.5	11.4	12.5	12.5
25 mos. to 3 yrs.	23.1	13.8	10.6	14.1
37 mos. to 5 yrs.	30.8	17.4	14.9	18.8
Longer than 5 yrs.	26.9	42.5	12.8	34.1
Total	100.0	100.0	100.0	100.0

The patterns revealed in table 5–14 should be matched with those demonstrated in table 5–15 to see how deeply imbedded these styles of life had become over a period of years. Thus, 34.1 percent of all respondents had been on their own for five years or more; 18.8 percent between three and five years; and only 17.4 percent one year or less.

Table 5–14 shows that black street people were geographically more stable than whites. Women, who tended to be younger, had most recently left home and were both the most transient and the most stable members of the street population. It would seem that they either dug in wherever they happened to be or rapidly moved on.

Contact with Parents

Few street people were currently receiving any financial support from their parents or relatives. But most of them, 79.7 percent, had maintained at least some tenuous contact with their parents—an occasional phone call or letter, often in times of severe distress. Going "home," however, did not appear to be a viable option for these young people. Although almost one-half (48.5 percent) said that their parents would allow them to come home and live with them, a mere 6.5 percent of the subjects expressed any intention or desire to do so. It seems that, for better or worse, street people were on their own.

Mental Hospitalization

Nearly one in four members of the sample (22 percent) admitted to having spent at least some time in a mental hospital. Of those who had a history of hospitalization, one-fifth (20.7 percent) had been admitted at least twice, and one-fourth (25.9 percent) had been hospitalized for six months or more. The mental hospitalization rate for blacks (37 percent) was considerably higher than for white males (22.5 percent) or for white females (14.9 percent). In addition, it should be noted that with few exceptions these mental hospitalizations occurred after the individual's departure from home.

Military Service

Fifty-two of the male respondents (23.1 percent of those men eighteen years or older who were U.S. citizens) had been in the military service, most in the army. Of those who had spent some time in the service, twenty (38.5 percent) had served in Vietnam. More than half (51.1 percent) of all discharged subjects were separated under less than honorable circumstances. Two of the respondents were, at the time of the study, still in the service—both were longtime AWOLs.

Police and the Courts

The street population had had a predictable experience with the criminal justice system. Of those eighteen years or older, 64.9 percent said that since becoming adults they had been arrested at least once. By and large these arrests had been for such misdemeanors as panhandling, vagrancy, shoplifting, or drug possession, but 12.4 percent of all adult respondents had been convicted of felonies, and 5.3 percent had spent at least one year in prison. Women had a comparatively "low" arrest rate (38.9 percent), and only one woman indicated that she had been convicted of a felony.

Drug Use

The use, possession, and sale of drugs was part and parcel of the life of street people and a frequent source of tension between them and law enforcement personnel. Marijuana was the most commonly used drug among street people, followed closely by beer and/or wine. Although less than half of the population was currently using LSD, a substantial percentage (18.1 percent) were "regular" LSD users. Methedrine use among street people was negligible, as was the use of cocaine—probably because of its high cost. Heroin addiction was not at that time widespread among street people. Only 1.2 percent of the subjects reported using heroin ten times or more during the previous month. However, an additional 6.4 percent reported that they had used it at least once during the survey month, and a total of 10.2 percent reported a history of heroin addiction in the past. What was obvious, however, was a pattern of drug usage much like that of the hippie era with its promiscuous experimentation in respect to all kinds of drugs.

Conclusions

What is one to make of these data, and how should the phenomenon be viewed?[13] The population of street people included

in the sample were a very marginal lot. In terms of affiliation to
social institutions, social capability, and psychosocial assets, they
were extremely deficient. In the jargon of the times—which could
be marvelously precise—they were the "least together," or the
"most out of it."

The most salient findings bear on the socioeconomic origins
and conditions of street people. What the sample revealed had
already been intuitively perceived by the staff of the area's social
agencies: the street person of 1974 was a qualitatively different
kind of human being than the hippie of 1967. The differences
were profound and should have laid to rest the pervasive myth
that he or she was a new version of the flower child. The logic
of that erroneous assumption held that the street person possessed similar attitudes, values, skills, ideology, and background.
The most unfortunate consequence of the error was the presumption that the poverty of the street person was self-imposed.

In the case of the hippie, that presumption was accurate—
at least until the great influx following the human be-in. Shortly
thereafter, as we have seen, the *person* changed; the ideology and
artifacts of the hippie culture remained, however, to influence
the wider society. We would expect the street person of 1974,
then, to embody certain of these ideological characteristics. Indeed, most American youth would be expected to have shared
the legacies of hippiedom. And so it seemed for the street person,
at least on the surface. At a deeper level, though, the data suggest
that the hippielike surface was superficial. The hippie had political beliefs, often voiced in terms of an articulated anarchism.
Street people's lives lacked political content: when pressed, they
might respond with "leftish" positions—but this was more a re-
flection of contemporary zeitgeist than of conviction. Further,
although the street person's drug involvement was quite intense,
it lacked any of the earlier quasi-religious context. The street
person used drugs to get high, to avoid boredom; the original
hippie used drugs as a means to achieve some kind of personal
awareness. For the hippie, communal living had been a conscious, willed experiment in new social forms; for the street person, communal living was a practical necessity characterized by
little interpersonal commitment of satisfaction. For the hippie,
panhandling represented a conscious decision not to work; for

the street person, panhandling was often the only way he or she could obtain the money necessary to survive.

These contrasts should not be construed to mean that the hippie was some pure, lovely, ideologically committed young person, and that the street person suffered by comparison. My point, really, is simple: by and large street people were not hippies. While there were certainly a few leftovers from the 1967 Haight-Ashbury district adrift on Telegraph Avenue in 1974, they were exceptions.

A very real poverty was the hallmark of the street person. The data are quite compelling on this score. Whereas the hippie was the child of the affluent middle class, the street person was the child of the working class. His or her parents were hard-working people whose trappings of affluence were heavily mortgaged. The street person did not really have the luxury of wiring home to mom or dad for money. Parents may have responded on occasion to such a call, but they were in no position to afford the upkeep of a chronically dependent child. In addition, the psychological strain between parent and child was such that the affiliative conditions for continued financial support did not exist. The street person, in terms of both financial and emotional needs, was on his or her own.

But "being on one's own" was not an unusual situation for youth. The American ethos held that young people did leave the family nest—more than that, they were expected to make their own way in the world. It was at this point that the street person came face to face with an insuperable problem: how was he or she to make his or her own way? The conventional path, indeed the socially required path, was by way of the occupational structure.

In recent times entrance into the primary labor force and accomplishment therein has required extensive involvement in the educational process. We have seen that street people were school dropouts. Fully one-third never completed high school; only 6 percent completed a two-year college degree, and only 9 percent graduated from a four-year institution. A generation earlier such data would have been commonplace and not particularly relevant to ultimate labor force involvement and success. But by 1974, when even college graduates had begun to have difficulty finding employment, street people were faced with grim and ominous occupational futures. Street people were, with few exceptions, unemployed and, more significantly, unemployable in the context of the labor market as it existed at that time. Their work histories, when they had worked at all, were testaments to economic superfluity. Their employment had been part-time, unskilled, erratic, or episodic in nature. Most were dependent on a casual labor market that was fast disappearing. The sad fact was that they had little in the way of vocational skills. Without social graces or presentable attire, let alone employee references, they had few if any marketable attributes to help them achieve reasonable employment.

The street person would have worked if he or she could. It was a compelling finding that so many of the subjects indicated not only a need for, but a wish for, conventional employment. And it must be remembered that they did not express grandiose occupational aspirations. They were not seeking employment as physicists, architects, or executives—they sought unskilled work (although they may not have been happy with such a limitation). Nearly 35 percent said that they "will take any job they can get"! This was not the response of the jaded counterculturist. It was, indeed, more akin to the response one would get if sampling the unemployed of the Great Depression era, and it came, in many cases, from subjects who had experienced several years of constant and relentless rejection by prospective employers. One might think that they would have turned, in bitterness, from any willingness at all to be employed.

The street person had arrived at this desperate point for a variety of reasons. For some there were serious family problems; for others there may well have been real limitations in psychological and intellectual equipment; for most there seems to have been a subliminal or barely articulated knowledge that "making it" in America, given their condition, had become more fantasy than reality. To serve an educational apprenticeship of some sixteen years requires discipline and purpose, but also requires some sense that the effort will lead to something. The mystique of the late 1960s did not encourage such an attitude, and the realities of the job market made the notion of a liberal arts education as occupational preparation seem ludicrous. The official unemployment rate—for half a decade—had hovered between 5 and 6 percent; for youth it had been much higher. Teenagers, for example, had a rate of unemployment between 15 and 20 percent. And these were official rates, which minimized the realities of part-time employment, underemployment, and labor force disaffiliation.

In short, the street people were cut off from this country's primary source of personal income. The most distinctive and public features of their life-style followed from this overriding fact. Stylistically, the street people responded to their plight in ways consistent with time-honored tradition. They did what socially marginal people had done throughout the centuries: they scrounged, they hustled, they begged, they stole—in a phrase, they tried very hard to survive. Therefore, we see the dramatic resemblance between these people and those of previous generations: the vagrant, the tramp, the hobo, and the derelict. All shared a legacy of near or real poverty; they all had had the superficial attributes of self-sufficiency and, hence, were cast among the unworthy poor, and all had been marked by their inability to make it by acceptable means.

The welfare apparatus of this society was not attuned to the survival needs of youth, because welfare in Western societies has never been attuned to the needs of the able-bodied poor. Welfare, rather, was geared to providing for those who in other times were called the "worthy poor," the disabled, the blind, the aged, and dependent children. The street people were very similar to the "sturdy beggars" of Elizabethan England. Superficially, they possessed the attributes of self-sufficiency; hence, the benefits of philanthropic and welfare concern were denied them.

Thus, they survived—of necessity—outside the bounds of a formal social welfare system as well as a formal occupational structure. Unskilled, their employment was haphazard. Street people, like hoboes, sought out geographic locations that afforded some small measure of opportunity, hospitality, or, at least, tolerance. Within these areas they carved out their version of the hoboes' "jungles" to protect themselves from the urban landscape. Street people chose the periphery of college campuses to establish their special kind of society. In the cities and towns across the country that housed major residential colleges and universities, colonies of street people could be found. Sometimes, as in Berkeley's People's Park in 1972, they even created tent cities. More often, they preempted certain restaurants, coffee shops, cafes, and some public facilities as their own. While college towns, because of their high youth density, afforded a modest measure of acceptance, the street people did not really interact with students; the street person was, even in a community of youth, a young outsider.

The data show how extremely transient street people were: almost one-third of the subjects had been in Berkeley less than one month; only 25 percent had been there over a year. At any moment they could as readily be found in Cambridge, Madison, Ann Arbor, or even along the Southern California coast from Santa Barbara to San Diego. Their life-styles in these other locations was similar to what was found in Berkeley: they panhandled, borrowed from "wealthier" peers, engaged in petty theft and small-time dope dealing. They slept and ate when and where they could, but if fortunate or creative enough a few established sufficient residential permanence to receive food stamps or some other form of public assistance. It was an unenviable life. For the poor, energy becomes focused on the requisites of survival: where to sleep, where to eat—and, to take the edge off these requirements—where and how to buy drugs or alcohol. It was understandable, then, that even the casual observer of street people was impressed (or depressed) by the number of twenty-year-olds who appeared far older.

With regard to social, and even ecological, attributes, street people resembled another well-known vagrant group: skid-row habitués. The differences between the old skid rows and the newer "youth ghettos" were not profound—with one decisive exception: the age of the residents.[14] Skid row had been a terminus for the impoverished, marginal man who was entering his late middle age; the youth ghetto was populated by teenagers and young men and women in their twenties. The youth ghetto, or at least its substratum of street people, also represented a terminus and, thus, the problem was truly of tragic dimensions. The street people of the 1970s were a mirror of the old historical vagrant, compounded by new and unique elements—a widespread and visceral disillusionment, pervasive then among youth, with the very fabric of social life; a demanding, rigorous educational apprenticeship that bore less and less on students' emotional or occupational needs; and the attenuation of familial and geographic ties.

The pathos of the street person is best conveyed by the note attached to one of the questionnaires of the Berkeley study, the comments of one respondent, a man of twenty-six:

> I'm a very lonely person who feels very humble here when I come to eat here. This project is of a priceless value to poor people in Berkeley. I wish I had the nerve to volunteer here for work. I feel sorry for myself a lot, but at least I know I can come here to eat when I'm hungry. I wish I could meet a girl because I haven't made love in almost a year. If only we had men in power who had the same feelings toward people as you people who are reading this: then we would have true peace and love. Long live the people who do the work of the Berkeley Emergency Food Project! I love you all.

With a constricting economy there was every reason to believe that the problem would grow.

UPI/Bettmann Newsphotos

6

The Contemporary
Homeless

T HE emergence of the hippie phenomenon occurred at the
very apogee of American economic power and well-being.
In the twenty years following the end of World War II this
country achieved a dominance over the world's economic affairs
that was unprecedented in its history and paralleled, perhaps,
only by the ancient Roman Empire and the recent British Empire.[1] By the end of World War II the great industrial powers
of Western Europe either lay in ruins or were exhausted and
bankrupt by six years of all-consuming conflict. The cities of
Japan were a wasteland of char and rubble. The United States,
alone, was left with its stupendous industrial might unscathed
and intact; it was in an unchallengeable position to command
global markets and enrich itself beyond the imaginations of its
citizens who had so recently cowered under the awful shadow
of the Great Depression.

Unemployment had all but disappeared during the war. The
rate had been 14.6 percent in 1940 but had fallen to an amazing
1.9 percent by 1945. With the end of defense production and
the discharge of several million men from the armed services,
unemployment rose quickly but never climbed much over 5.5
percent until the economic events of the 1970s. Weekly earnings
had quadrupled between 1940 and 1963, rising from $24.96 to
$99.38. In *real* and constant dollars, this change represented an
increase of 100 percent in wages for the employed. Gross national
product had increased fourfold and national income by a factor

of five. Per capita income had risen from $595 in 1940 to $2,366 in 1962. Family income rose commensurately. Prices did rise during those years, of course, but at a relatively modest rate: the purchasing power of the dollar fell from an index of 204.9 in 1940 to 93.7 in 1963 (1957–59 = 100). The wealth of individuals, like that of the nation as a whole, showed a substantial *real* gain.[2]

By practically all measures times had been good. School enrollment was up because of the baby boom; more significantly, enrollment in colleges and universities had increased from 1,494,000 in 1940 to 2,279,000 in 1960, and to a whopping 6,065,000 by 1970. The nascent labor force was becoming more educated. But behind this newfound affluence that affected so many American families hid a shadow of more difficult and stringent life. Indeed, the population of the United States was in the process of splitting into two very different worlds: one of relative fortune and prosperity—large in numbers, secure, and well paid; the other living in or near poverty.

The rediscovery of poverty in America can in some measure be attributed to Michael Harrington, whose *The Other America* signaled a swell of concern for those who had been left out of the economic bonanza.[3] From the end of World War II until 1960, the rate of absolute poverty in this country had remained distressingly constant at a figure, depending upon the estimator, of between 20 and 25 percent.[4] The nation's absolute standard of poverty came to be defined, ultimately, in rather stringent terms: the cost of a basket of food required in order to maintain a subsistence level of nutrition, multiplied by a factor of three to allow for other necessities of life such as clothes and housing, and then reduced by some 25 percent.[5] This Orshansky standard, adjusted for rises in the consumer price index, family size, and its urban or rural status, remains to this day the national "poverty level" threshold. In 1960 the number of people living below that level was 39,851,000, or some 22.2 percent of the total population.

The extent of poverty, defined in *relative* terms, had not changed much either during the course of those expansive years. Thus, the ratio of mean income of the poorest one-fifth of people to the means of all families was 0.25 in 1947, and exactly the same in 1963.[6] From a slightly different vantage point, in 1947 the poorest one-fifth of families received but 5 percent of total family income; in 1963 they fared exactly the same.[7] The poor, contemplating their economic status relative to the rest of the country, were no better off in 1963 than they had been in 1947.

In the early 1960s almost one in every four Americans lived in a state of poverty, officially defined in a way calculated to provide only a bare minimum of subsistence. Obviously, there had been an improvement since the bleak days of the Great Depression when it was thought that "one third of the nation was ill-fed, ill-housed, and ill-clothed." But, in the early 1960s, the numbers were nonetheless perceived as shameful—even shocking—for such a rich and opulent society.

The paradox of a large mass of poor people living in a country characterized by a robust economy was not difficult to comprehend: the new wealth was moving toward those who had advantages, either in respect to location in the more blessed part of the labor force or in respect to an accumulated capital. Neither of these two facets of economic privilege were independent of some compelling demographic facts. First, there was the problem of race. Nonwhite individuals and families carried a disproportionate share of the burden of poverty. For example, the overall unemployment rate in 1963 was 5.7 percent; for white members of the labor force it was 5.1, but for nonwhites, it was more than 10.9 percent. Racial inequality in regard to opportunities for employment was compounded by a similar inequality in earnings. In 1959, for example, black family income was only 51 percent that of white families. Moreover, although the total poverty rate in 1960 was 22.2 percent, for whites as a subgroup the rate was 17.8 percent, but for blacks as a subgroup it was a staggering 55.1 percent.[8]

But the fact that nonwhites, particularly blacks, were more prone to be poor did not really require the proof of elegant statistical analysis; a trip to the great urban ghettos would have been enough to convince the skeptic that a grim economic inequality was gestating behind the booming might of American industry.

Another significant poverty factor was gender. Women were becoming more likely to be found among the poor than were men. A profound trend, continuing to this day, of an increase in the numbers of households headed by women, whether through divorce, separation, accident, or choice, was one root cause of this gender and poverty linkage. Another trend, no doubt partly determined by the first, was increasing numbers of women entering the labor force. The unemployment rates for women always ran higher than those for men: in 1963 it was 6.5 percent for females and 5.2 percent for males. And, just as blacks earned less than whites, wages for women were considerably less than for their male counterparts—indeed women's paychecks reflected only 60 percent of the monies earned by men in 1963.[9] The phenomenon of single mothers disadvantaged in the labor force was reflected in the official poverty data: 48.9 percent of female-headed families lived below the poverty threshold in 1960.

Other demographic statistics that served to explicate the extent of poverty in America in those years concerned age and geography. Young people, as always, were more subject to the vicissitudes of labor force participation and, in those years, the aged were in a sorry plight. Finally, all was not well on the farm: rural people were much more likely to fall into the depths of poverty than their urban fellows.

Thus, at the very time the hippie began his brief flirtation with poverty, there existed simultaneously an unprecedented economic wealth and a large fraction of the population who lived in poverty by force of circumstance. Their condition had been untouched by the economic expansion of nearly two decades, and their presence challenged the goodwill of the country. Then was born the great War on Poverty, a product of a martyred president, his successor Lyndon Johnson, their political party, and a civil rights movement that aroused the compassion of a more advantaged citizenry. But this effort, despite some very real gains, would end in failure.

Massive grants of federal monies to the various states and communities of the nation resulted in the expansion of welfare programs to cover many more categories of the needy. Eligibility requirements for the old programs were loosened to the extent that many more people could avail themselves of monies, goods, and services. The theoretical orientation of the War on Poverty was evident in its primary organ of administration: the Office of Economic Opportunity (OEO). The government's guiding assumption was that poverty was a function of a lack of *opportunity;* its elimination, consequently, depended in large measure on the provision of opportunity for those excluded from gainful employment. Education, job training, and the removal of barriers that hindered or totally excluded blacks, women, and other disadvantaged groups from various labor markets were the heart and soul of OEO programs. For those unable to join the labor force—children, the aged, the handicapped, and the chronically ill—somewhat more generous welfare benefits were provided or encouraged. In the prevailing spirit of the civil rights movement, the ideology of community action and participation provided the ambiance for much of what was done or contemplated.

Significant reductions in the numbers of poor people occurred following the implementation of antipoverty legislation. Thus, the poverty rate dropped from 19.0 percent in 1964, when the legislation was enacted, to its low point of 11.1 percent in 1973.[10] This percentage drop represented an *absolute* reduction of some thirteen million people but there still remained twenty-three million who lived in poverty. Much of the reduction that had occurred, moreover, could be attributed to the rise in welfare benefits; large numbers of people were no longer *officially* poor even though they still lived on the dole.

Training people for jobs that were becoming less available either through technologically determined obsolescence or through changes in the basic structure of the American economy may have contributed little to reducing poverty. Apocryphal stories about armies of newly trained welders competing for fewer and fewer jobs were common during the heyday of the poverty wars. The problem of poverty obviously was more complex and profound than a limited opportunity structure. The nation was dividing into two very distinct populations: the relatively affluent middle classes, equipped with the skills, adaptability, and social capabilities for succeeding in the labor market, and an "underclass" of unskilled, poorly educated unemployed, subemployed, or marginally employed who were more or less *permanently* barred from entry into the first category.

The idea of a "secondary labor force" is not new, as we have seen; it is our friend the residuum with some very special features derived from the nature of the United States in the context of the late twentieth century. David M. Gordon lists some of these features as they appear in the context of the ghetto:

> A variety of additional labor market characteristics [in the central city] joined "unemployment" as symptoms of labor market disadvantage. For many workers in the ghetto, unemployment seemed a small component of a much broader syndrome of connected labor market difficulties. Problems like low wages, job instability, menial work, low skills, poor worker motivation, discrimination, poor job information, and inadequate job access seemed equally to demand attention. Each problem seemed somehow causally related to the others. If you had one problem, you were likely to suffer from some of the others as well. . . .
>
> Increasingly, a concept of underemployment replaced unemployment at the core of manpower policy formulation, encompassing most of these new symptoms.[11]

Later yet, *subemployment* was to become the word of choice for a concept more complex than simple "unemployment."

Gordon's characterization of the secondary labor force could extend beyond the inner-city ghetto; it was *not* a notion based on race, although nonwhites were particularly good candidates for membership. It is important to note that the theory of the dual labor market is not a conception that economists use to portray *character;* we are not dealing with the psychology of misfits. Rather, it is a conception that addresses the structure of economies; specifically, the nature of contemporary labor markets. But the relationship between the personal attributes of people and the characteristics of labor markets is reciprocal:

> With few exceptions, these jobs [of the secondary sector] were typically menial, requiring little mental or physical dexterity. Instability of the work force seemed not only to be accepted by employers in these job categories but often encouraged by them. The jobs paid low wages and conferred minimal status. The quality of working conditions was poor. Most important, apparently, the jobs seemed completely isolated. They were not connected to job ladders of any sort. No matter how long an

employee worked at these jobs or how clearly he demonstrated his diligence or skill, there seemed to be no fixed channels through which he could rise above his original job.[12]

Many jobs in the secondary market by their very nature are unstable and, hence, generate an instability and unreliability in their incumbents. Some jobs are found in the secondary market not so much because they "belong" there by virtue of the intrinsic nature of the work but by virtue of institutional evolution: "Work normally performed in the primary sector is sometimes shifted. to the secondary sector through subcontracting, temporary help services, recycling of new employees through probationary periods and so on."[13]

In short, the complex texture of the evolving economy has led to the generation of a secondary job market that is, for all practical purposes, walled off from the primary market and that tends to foster in its employees those very traits of work habit and attitude that allow it to function cheaply and, for its purposes, efficiently. For the jobholder, the secondary market reinforces those attributes of behavior that landed him there to begin with. The cycle is vicious and intractable.

It should not be surprising that with the solidification of the dual labor market there would arise a new generation of vagrant and homeless. The street people were harbingers of that sad resurrection. The homeless of the 1990s are its fruition. From its low point of 11.1 percent in 1973, the poverty rate has crept upward, reaching 15.2 percent in 1983. In 1987 it stood at 13.5 percent of all persons; this percentage represents some 32,546,000 people living below what is essentially an emergency level of subsistence. These overall rates conceal enormous differences between subpopulations. Table 6–1 shows the great disparity between blacks and whites as well as the creep in magnitude of poverty since the heyday of America's boom.

If we consider the serious plight of female-headed households with children under age eighteen, demonstrated in table 6–2, the segmentation of society into "haves" and "have-nots" becomes more apparent and more chilling.

A consideration of the extent of poverty in respect to the question of homelessness is obviously not a digression; it is the

Table 6–1
Poverty Rates by Race (Persons)

	Whites	Blacks	All
1987	10.5%	31.8%	13.5%
1973	8.4	30.9	11.1
1959	18.1	54.9	22.4

Source: U.S. Bureau of the Census, *Poverty in the U.S., 1987,* Current Population Reports, Series P-60, no. 163 (Washington, D.C.: U.S. Government Printing Office, 1989).

Table 6–2
Poverty Rates by Race for Female Households with Children

	White Fem Households	Black Fem Households	All Fem Households
1987	38.7%	59.5%	46.1%
1973	35.2	58.8	43.2
1959	51.7	N.A.	59.9

Source: U.S. Bureau of the Census, *Poverty in the U.S., 1987,* Current Population Reports, Series P-60, no. 163 (Washington, D.C.: U.S. Government Printing Office, 1989).

whole point. People of means, with rare and trivial exceptions, do *not* become homeless. Poor people are the group at risk of becoming homeless; when their poverty occurs in a time of explosive housing costs their risk of homelessness becomes acute.

There is some question as to whether the real and practical availability of housing units in this country has actually diminished over the last decade; some have even been willing to argue that in terms of such exotic indices as square footage of accommodation per capita, or the numbers of bathrooms per housing unit, or the bedroom space per child, America's housing base has never been so good. It is probably true that the overall quality of housing has improved over recent years. But surely these observations are far off the real point, which revolves around the ability of poor people to purchase shelter in the open market. That ability has been severely curtailed. Home ownership is, of course, out of the question for the nation's poor, as it is for increasing numbers of the middle classes. Cheap rents is the housing issue for the poor and the near poor. The concept, like poverty itself, can be relative but for the absolutely poor the price of rent is an absolute crisis. Single room occupancies (SROs), one of the mainstays of the impoverished, have diminished in number.[14] Further, the consumer price index for rents has increased over recent years at a rate much higher than the overall average and is exceeded only by the rise in cost of medical care.[15] This last consideration, by the way, makes the Orshansky standard of poverty not only archaic but perverse. Rent has long since surpassed food as the most expensive budgetary cost. In any event, while the numbers of poor people have increased, the numbers of "cheap" rentals have declined.[16]

The experience of the federally funded Section 8 Program, which provides rent subsidies to selected tenants, provides further evidence that all is not well in the matter of housing for those on the edge of disaster. "Under that program, households selected by local housing authorities are required to find housing that meets certain quality standards and that rents for no more than a specified 'fair market rent.' Despite the large subsidy available under the program, the majority of households selected are unable to find housing that qualifies within a two month time limit and must forego benefits. Single-parent families have been particularly unsuccessful in finding housing under the program."[17]

The contemporary scene is marked by a growth in the numbers of people trapped in the secondary labor force at the same time that the supply of affordable shelter diminishes. One serious consequence is the new visibility of homeless people and the latest flurry of attention that this unhappy band has received over the last six centuries. The attention, today, is relatively sympathetic compared to that which was focused on the homeless in times past; it is, in fact, much like that which occurred during the depression era. Now, as then, we find a news media that portrays the phenomenon in the tradition of a muckraking—"look at the awful things that are happening in America"—and a body politic that cautiously joins in the chorus of indignation and even empathy. At the same time, however, the old stigma of the homeless

continues to be reinforced—without the literal branding sometimes used in the past, of course, but with the hot iron of twen-
tieth-century social science.

The historical response to the vagrant, we know, has been
harsh, unsympathetic, and—all too often—downright draconian
in its severity. We have seen how he could be whipped, branded,
jailed, transported, indentured, enslaved, or executed; in less
harsh times, he was scorned, shunned, harassed, or pushed out
of the community. Today, the vilification of the homeless is
couched in a language of surface neutrality: he or she is "mentally
ill," "alcoholic," "drug addicted," "pauperized." What is there
about the vagrant soul that calls forth this reaction from the
good members of society?

First, the historical vagrant has invariably been found on the
fringes of criminality. He lives when he is in town—whether in
the slums of London, Paris, Chicago, or New York—in the seedy
and decaying parts of the urban metropolis. His immediate as-
sociates are thieves, drug dealers, prostitutes, panderers, and
hoodlums. Indeed, sometimes the vagrant is also a criminal. But
even when he obeys the laws and never gets into trouble with
the authorities, he is still suspect because of where he lives and
who his neighbors are. Why does he gravitate to such unwhole-
some parts of the city? He cannot afford to live elsewhere. He
lives within the decaying part of the city because it is the only
place that he is allowed to live. It is in fact the one place wherein
the police authorities collect, by default, all of the disreputable
peoples of the metropolis. It has always been so.

But the vagrant suffers from more than guilt by association.
The vagrant lives by his wits, and expediency often requires him
to break the law or—at the very least—to overstep the boundaries
of acceptable behavior. Vagrants are often reduced to begging,
but begging, as the historical record for the past several hundred
years demonstrates, is frowned upon by the establishment. Begging is an ancient, but never really honorable, craft. The beggar
presents an immediate moral problem to those he begs from:
the potential donor must decide whether he is worthy to receive
alms or an unworthy swindler. This problem is at the root of
most of the legislation concerning begging. It remains the decisive policy question of the present. The historical beggar was

ingenious; Henry Mayhew offers a lengthy catalog of the deceptions, frauds, and scams devised by people as they preyed upon the sympathy of a confused and annoyed citizenry. But Mayhew's conniving beggars, despite their various ploys, were truly needy. The ubiquitous tale of the wealthy beggar is a fiction, a persistent fiction.

A second source of the vagrant's disrepute is the debauched life society at large presumes him or her to lead. His or her dissolution is supposed to stem from fondness for drink. Ribton-Turner notes that the establishment's concern with vagrants and their abuse of spirits goes back to at least A.D. 1285 when an ordinance imposing a curfew on ale houses was promulgated by Edward I. The intent, so familiar to modern ears, was to interdict the supply of the noxious substance.

The impoverished drunk is, of course, the prototypical figure of America's skid rows. He is the Bowery bum. Whereas the hobo travels and works, and the tramp travels and does not work, the bum neither travels nor works. He stays put because of his infirmity or his age in an area of last resort where there is cheap food, cheap lodging, cheap wine, and a relatively tolerant police force. The hallmarks of skid row used to be the flophouse, where shelter could be obtained for a pittance, and the mission, where a meal of sorts could be bought for the price of listening to a sermon on the dangers of alcohol or the prospects for damnation.

Skid row, in its traditional form, has disappeared in the wake of urban redevelopment and gentrification. The bum has joined a much larger population of vagrants and homeless whose stomping grounds no longer have the tidy geographic boundaries of the old skid rows. The blending of the bum with this wider society and the dispersion of all vagrants throughout the city has made alcoholism appear a more ubiquitous phenomenon than it really is among the homeless. While current analysis generally holds that the homeless suffer from severe problems with alcohol, alcoholism is probably true only for that part of the larger whole which, just a few years ago, would have been called the bums. Alcohol use is a feature of contemporary adult life. It is "a problem of the homeless" only because of its visibility (the homeless drink in public) and because conservative moralists hold that those living in poverty should not drink. In other words, the millionaire commits no sin while drinking his rare vintages, the respectable member of the middle class does nothing wrong when he sips his martini, and the hardworking blue-collar laborer is not at fault for desiring a cold beer or two, but a homeless person who seeks the solace of a cheap half-pint is reprehensible.[18]

A word should be said about the abuse of other substances, notably drugs. It is an interesting fact that drug abuse—and specifically the use of morphine and other opium derivatives— has often been a feature of modern vagrant and neoantinomian life. Opium, we have seen, was used in the working quarters of nineteenth-century Manchester and among the shanties of gold-possessed San Francisco. And, of course, hoboes often used opium. Their involvement with hard drugs was in part a function of the promiscuous use of morphine by the surgeons of the Civil War. Among the many restless and uprooted veterans of that fratricide were addicted young people, some of whom went West to become the prototypical hoboes. Much of the contemporary and near-contemporary cant of the drug culture, terms like "junkie" and "hophead," were originally hobo terms for their drug-using brethren. The homeless veterans of Vietnam, too, have often turned to drug use. Again, the estimates of habitual use vary. Among today's homeless, veterans of *all* wars contribute 18 percent of the total homeless population in St. Louis and 51 percent in Baltimore. Of these, veterans of the Vietnam conflict comprise anywhere from 32 to 47 percent.[19] Thus, approximately one-third of one-third of the homeless consist of Vietnam-era veterans. Drug abuse among all homeless runs at from 10 to 33 percent of the total homeless and occurs more frequently among the younger people (unlike alcohol abuse, which is more likely to be found among the older of the homeless).[20] Thus, of all drug abusers, an important fraction consists of Vietnam veterans.

Alcohol and drug abuse are not the only characteristics presumed to characterize the vagrant life. The public at large has always assumed that vagrants practice sexual license. Vagrants are generally believed to be promiscuous at best, and criminally perverted at worst. Whenever a sex crime is committed, the police invariably turn to the vagrant population for suspects.

Mental illness, whether real or feigned, is another characteristic of the vagrant that adds to his disrepute. The wandering fool is always on the scene, more usually as a target of derision than as a subject of charity. An enormous amount of attention has been given, in the literature on vagrancy, to the mad vagrant, and more particularly to the madman imposter. If authentically demented vagrants did not exist, however, where would the fraudulent madmen (and women) learn methods for impersonating the mentally ill? Despite the large numbers of alleged pretenders exposed and punished by the authorities over the centuries, are not mentally ill vagrants common today, and would they not have been even more prevalent in the past? Given any establishment's suspicions concerning the innate sinfulness of the vagrant population, probably many supposed "frauds" were truly ill. The delicate diagnostic task of separating the true sufferer from the malingerer is a problem that even modern science has not solved.

The descriptive language for the mad vagrant is rich, indeed. William Langland's famous medieval poem *Piers Plowman* describes the mad vagrant c. 1370 as one who "wanders about, more or less mad, according to the phases of the moon. These care for no cold, nor reckon aught of heat, and move after the moon, wandering without money, over many wide countries, without understanding, but with no evil intent." The phony lunatic, whose dementia did have an evil intent, was called an "Abraham's man," feigning madness in order to extract a copper or two from the unwary. In Germany he was called a *vopper;* in Italy he was among the *spiritati.* Sometimes the insane vagrant included the epileptic and what we would now call the mentally deficient. Whatever he was called, the mentally disturbed vagrant has been a permanent fixture among the dispossessed people of the world.

The argument that a substantial segment of homeless people today consist of the mentally ill who have been evicted, so to speak, from the protection of the mental hospital is likely to be true—up to a point. We have seen that nearly 25 percent of the street people of the 1970s admitted to spending some time in a mental hospital. Various studies confirm that many homeless of

the 1980s share a history of hospitalization or institutionalization
for mental illness. The exact percentage depends on the inves-
tigator and, not unimportantly, on the criteria invoked for defining mental illness. The numbers range from 20 percent to 60
percent, but the latter estimate sounds extravagant.[21] Whether
that proportion is any larger today than it was in prior historical
eras is unclear. After all, most mentally ill people of the past had
never been in mental hospitals or their historical equivalent. The
mentally ill were part of the world of vagrancy in the thirteenth
century and in every century since. But though a *part* of that
unhappy community, they never were characteristic of it.

A fourth element in the vagrant's bad reputation is his association with ethnically or racially stigmatized and despised
groups. This is nowhere more clear than in the case of the Irish
vagrant of the late 1840s who flocked to the cities of England
during and after the Great Famine. Poor and Catholic, Celtic in
body features rather than Saxon, Irish vagrants were singled out
for a special contempt. Thus, one of Mayhew's informants could
indignantly claim that "the Irish are mostly filthy and diseased.
They live upon little or nothing, and upon the worst kind of
provision that can be bought, even though it be not fit for human
food. They will eat anything. The Irish tramp lives solely by
begging."[22] The Catholic Irishman was Protestant England's version of America's black: lazy, inferior, and dangerous.

Gypsies were another group that attracted special contempt.
They dressed differently, they were dark-skinned, they were
believed to be swindlers, thieves, and kidnappers of children.
Their bad reputation carried throughout Europe. Like the Jews,
they were singled out by the authorities and the general population for harsh treatment—the latest example being their liq-
uidation through gassing in the extermination camps of World
War II.

In the past, the American hobo and tramp were usually white.
The occasional black hobo or tramp in the vagrants' world was
usually subjected to the same kinds of discrimination that characterized the wider society. The black vagrant was, in a very real
sense, an outcast among outcasts. His numbers were somewhat
larger in the community of bums found in the skid-row areas of
the cities, where, especially in the West, he or she was joined by

Indian vagrants. The racial integration of American life that has occurred over the last two decades has brought with it a concomitant integration within the world of vagrancy and homelessness. Ironically, the black man and woman are now free to join the visible homeless where their numbers now seem to comprise anywhere between one-third and one-half of the people who are without shelter.[23] Like the Irish and the Gypsy, blacks must endure a special stigma because they belong to a denigrated racial group.

A fifth characteristic of the vagrant homeless is his status as an unattached human being, separated from, if not totally lacking, close family and kin. The binding of human beings to one another through ties of blood and marriage has always been seen as a defining feature of our species; in that sense the isolated individual is, by definition, inhuman. It is impossible to overstate the tremendous importance of family ties in the social and psychological life of conventional society; it is equally impossible to overstate the suspicion and even fear that those without family ties provoke among the orthodox. It is as though the vagrant's mere existence was an affront, perhaps even an attack, on the fundamental institution of family life.

The appearance of being cut off, in a self-inflicted manner, from family bonds may belie the reality. It is a difficult empirical problem because the appearance is obviously correct: the vagrant *is* alone. But large numbers of vagrants *do* maintain contact with their kin. The contact may be sporadic and inconsistent; or it may include periods of close contact alternating with periods of separation; it is very frequently, as in the case of the migratory laborer, accompanied by the forwarding of monies to feather the distant nest. The sending of a proportion of one's wages back to a more stationary family can go on for decades, as was the case in the United States of the Chinese laborers imported to do the dirty work of tunneling through the Sierras, or in Great Britain of the despised Irishman living in Liverpool, Bristol, or London who sent back what he could to his wife and children. There are many similar examples—the record of such durability in attachment is profound and inspiring.

Or contact may indeed be absent altogether. But whether actual or only apparent, disaffiliation from his family has always served to single the vagrant out for a unique opprobrium and distaste. His very life was subversive. The homeless, today, yield a subpopulation that may be unique: the unattached mother with child or children. Critics point to this new phenomenon with outrage, expressing their scorn for what is claimed to be a generation of loose women who spawn children without regard for their care or the sensibilities of the wider community. The "bag lady," of course, was a well-known, though relatively rare, feature of the old homeless population. Today's women, however, with children in tow, comprise a major proportion of the homeless who occupy the various shelters and hostels that have been improvised within our cities. They also can be found in a variety of refuges for battered women. The Committee on Health Care for Homeless People claims that up to 28 percent of all homeless consist of homeless families, almost all headed by a female. The stigma attached to such families is only compounded when they also happen to be black.

Still another characteristic of the traditional vagrant is his youth. Vagabondage, like crime or substance abuse, is not usually for older people, for the life is much too hard. The "retired" vagrant becomes, as I have suggested, a bum—that is, if he survives long enough to enjoy that condition. But the decision to pick up and go someplace where there might be easier pickings is invariably the kind of choice that occurs to young people, particularly men as yet unencumbered by wife, children, and career, and hence with not much to lose by taking off. The people who make such choices are often *really* young.

We have seen that the conventional image of the grizzled and cantankerous miner, the forty-niner with mule and pickax, was an erroneous image. He was more likely to have been a teenager. And so too was the cowboy, the lumberman, and the member of the railroad gang. It was the adolescent who took to the roads and became the highwayman and bandit. Billy the Kid was typical. Although Captain Kidd was middle-aged, his ships were probably manned by teenaged pirates. It is worth noting, too, that the guerrilla armies and terrorist bands of today are also manned predominantly by teenage boys and girls—some of them still on the threshold of puberty.

The distinction between vagrants and runaways is an artifact of late twentieth-century sophistication, as is the most recent reformulation that distinguishes between "runaways" and "throwaways." But whatever the nomenclature, the child wanderer is an ancient figure who eternally reappears in the sad history of dispossession. I am speaking now of *children* as opposed to adolescents. Homeless children roamed in packs throughout the streets of urban Europe in the Middle Ages and such children remain a feature of cities today. The sprawling urban environments of the developing world, cities such as São Paulo, Rio de Janeiro, and Mexico City, are overrun with bands of children surviving as best they can on the margins of legality. Closer to home, the child torn loose from hearth and family whether by discard or choice has been found in significant numbers on our own streets. Like his fellows in other countries and in other eras he is a problem to police and to philanthropy. Waifs, street Arabs, urchins, and mudlarks alike survive by means of theft, prostitution, violence, and whatever else they can think of themselves or be forced into by others more powerful than themselves. The contemporary gang member and drug entrepreneur who hires children to deliver his drugs is a dangerous and terrifying variant on an old theme.

Finally, we reach the universal, necessary condition for vagrancy and homelessness: the indispensable criterion of poverty. It might seem superfluous, even silly, to have to remind the reader that vagrant and homeless people are *poor,* but there has always been a strange disinclination to attribute the fact of homelessness to a lack of the money needed to purchase shelter. People of means are not really members of the homeless population even if they choose to wander about. They might be criminal, alcoholic, insane, or unattached—but they are not and cannot be homeless in any historic and intuitive sense.

Poverty and especially its more despised variant, pauperism, are conditions of stigma because of a historical social tendency to link the condition with some presumed moral failing or weakness within the afflicted individual. Even during the depths of the Great Depression, when it was obvious to all but the most dense that vast and uncontrollable economic forces were responsible for the millions thrown into poverty, people were ashamed of their poverty. And even if they saw themselves as victims and perhaps even saw their neighbors as similarly victimized by an unfeeling economy, they did not easily see strangers in the same generous light. It is a peculiar finding that while most poor people make an exception for themselves when they attempt to diagnose the malady of being poor, they are quick to join in the condemnation of many of their fellow poor issued by the populace at large.

The issue of course is not that homeless people are poor—a formulation that is a tautology. The question goes much deeper. Why are poor people poor? And why are some poor people homeless? A look at the rise and fall of the numbers of vagrant people will begin to throw some light on this matter.

Until very recent times the only evidence for the numbers of vagrant people derived from study of records left by government officials and the enactments of lawmakers. Needless to say, such records are often suspect, but they are the best we have. What is clear, however, is that although there has never been a time when vagrancy was ignored, there were times when it was attended to with more vigor. And these times were *always* either characterized by great economic distress or by its opposite, great economic expansion.

The great plague of 1349, as I have already noted, was one such instance. The decimation of the population of Europe created a great shortage of labor and, for the first time in that continent's history, men's labor was pegged to the price of labor in a semiopen marketplace. The villein could pick himself up and travel to a distant manor where he could negotiate a better wage—and there were manors aplenty to take him on. The former serf's freedom to choose his place of employment, and thereby his terms of employment, created a frenzy of anger and distress among the nobility. The Statute of Laborers was an attempt to keep people at home, where they belonged, and in the process control the escalation of wages. It didn't work; the lure of glorious possibility was too great. The years following the plague were good times for workers, and ambitious youth took to the road.

For several centuries Europe went through upheavals in its economy. Some of these upheavals were geographically localized, as when changes in the microclimate led to famine or armies moved across the land leaving devastation in their wake. Sometimes these upheavals were more general in nature, as with the steady and consistent movement toward an international and capitalist economy. Technology was a disrupter. And, of course, the opening of the New World to the exploitation of a turbulent Europe caused all sorts of changes. This latter event served as a great safety valve for society's malcontents and dispossessed, the people who either wanted something more than society provided or could not cope in their society.

Each time circumstance drove people from their traditional homes because of their appalling need or each time circumstances pulled people away from their traditional homestead because of the lure of greater possibility, the authorities engaged in a frenetic round of legislation to either stop the movement or to eliminate the mover. The punitive device of transportation was invented to cleanse the streets of London's vagrants—first, by shipping them off to the American colonies, and then, when that was no longer possible, to the desert continent of Australia. France, too, had its colonial repository for homeless pariahs, Cayenne, later to become that symbol of inhuman penal colonies, Devil's Island. And imperial Russia had the frigid vastness of Siberia to receive its undesirables.

The American migrator is in some respects a distinctive phenomenon. Mobility has been built into the ethos of our country; beginning in colonial times, the lure of virgin territories always a little further to the west caused people to pack up and move. The prospect of a better life was just beyond the next range of hills. From New England, Virginia, and the Carolinas people went across the Appalachians—first to the Cumberland, then to Ohio and Illinois, and then across the Mississippi into the Great Plains and beyond. Farming, in keeping with the agricultural character of the country, was the primary attraction, but the solitary could trap animals for furs. The mountain man became a folk hero; living alone for years at a time, thousands of miles from home, he collected his beaver pelts for sale to the fur companies who held periodic rendezvous in such places as Jackson Hole in the shadows of the Grand Tetons of Wyoming. Movement west, whether to farm or to trap, was a method of avoiding the economic hardship of staying put; if you failed to "make it" economically in one place, you could move on to another place. Thus America's ethos of mobility evolved and became legitimized.

The discovery of gold at Sutter's mill in 1848, like all subsequent gold strikes in other parts of the globe, attracted adventurers from all parts of the country and, indeed, the world. We have seen that many of these people were young and they came to California because their futures at home were perceived to be at best limited and at worst impossible.

The Civil War was a disrupting event at many levels. It created a subclass of sharecropping blacks; it also created a substantial group of dispossessed whites, many of whom moved to the West. What with the explosive growth of the railroads; the beginning of an important cattle industry; the existing gold mines and the later silver and copper mines; logging; and farming—the West promised unlimited possibilities for economic well-being. For most, it was a promise much overstated. The life was hard, but one could always move on. Back East, periodic economic depressions and recessions ensured that new cohorts of laborers would keep coming. Thus, the panic of 1873 saw a substantial increase in the numbers of wanderers and hoboes, as did the panic of 1893. Hard times at home coupled with the magnetic attraction of the West accounted for the periodic oscillations in the numbers of vagrant folk.

Eventually the historic role of the West was played out. The entire expanse of the United States began to act as an organic whole. The Great Depression of the 1930s was sad testimony to a national economy. The numbers of homeless reached stunning proportions. The migratory families typified by Steinbeck's Joads in his *The Grapes of Wrath* represented but a small fraction of people on the move or otherwise without shelter. Hunger was rampant and the breadline and the soup kitchen became the hallmarks of the Great Depression. Shantytowns, so bitterly called Hoovervilles by the inhabitants, could be found in most American cities. Made of cardboard, scrap sheet metals, canvas, and discarded lumber they were quickly erected and just as quickly destroyed by an irate and disturbed citizenry who would come, sometimes in the depths of night, to set them aflame. Very often it was the force of the state itself that put the torch to these makeshift communities of homeless.

The Great Depression was an awesome era. The streets, highways, and railroads of the country were filled with homeless people. Many young people took to the road, as they have always done, to look for opportunity and to spare their families the expense of another mouth to feed.

World War II absorbed almost all of these vagrants into the armed forces or wartime industry. Many blacks, former sharecroppers, moved to the labor-hungry industries of the North—to Detroit with its defense plants and to Richmond, California, with its shipyards. Almost anybody could get a job and almost everybody did. Vagrancy nearly disappeared and continued to remain a trivial feature of American society until the great economic expansion ceased and recessions began to reoccur once again. My historical outline is complete. We have now reached today's homeless and the familiar public outcry, legislative and philanthropic concern, food lines, and emergency shelters.

The linkage between a country's economy and its vagrancy problems is straightforward and inescapable. But it is confounded, throughout the record of history and in the analytic ruminations of today, by a strange inclination to tie homelessness to personal inadequacy or perversity. We have seen why this is so: stigma and disrepute, caused by a number of factors, adheres to the vagrant life. But the language that suggests the vagrant's disrepute has changed over the generations, and that shift in language reveals meaningful differences in the nature of public discourse surrounding the homeless. From "valiant beggar," the nomenclature of the fourteenth century, to "sturdy beggar," the common expression of Elizabethan England, to the "vagrant" of the last century, the "street people" of the 1970s, and the "homeless" of today, the terms have always implied an *unwillingness* to work on the part of those presumed to be capable of work. This evolution of language partially masks society's constant desire to discriminate between two categories of vagrant: the worthy poor and the unworthy poor.

Even in the darkest days of ignorance it was always acknowledged, somewhat begrudgingly, that there were some people whose poverty and need were beyond their own control. Cripples, the blind, the truly demented, orphans, and the elderly were exempted from the social expectation of exchanging labor for wages. Friars, monks, and others who did God's work, and students, too, were exempted from many restrictions. But these and other exceptions created chronic problems for society at large. How could society distinguish between a true blind man and someone who pretended to be blind; between an unfortunate cripple and one whose disability was a sham; between a lunatic and an Abraham's man; between a legitimate student and a fraudulent one? Modern politicians rant about "welfare fraud," but welfare fraud is not really a creation of the welfare state; rather it is a new term for a long-standing problem, one that is no more easily solved today than it was in those long past times.

Long ago the issue was who is worthy to receive alms? Everyone agreed that anyone capable of working who chose instead to subsist on charity was immoral. He who did not work because he would not work was morally flawed. It was as simple as that. The deficit was in their moral character. They took to drink and frolicked in the ale houses with their ill-gotten alms. While the upright ploughman worked hard and long for his sustenance, the sturdy beggar took advantage of the good folk of the realm; he scrounged and begged and stole and lied and cheated and did all of these things with a smirk on his face and a secret laugh at convention. If his fraud and deception were exposed, he surely deserved the branding, the imprisonment, the transportation, and the opprobrium of his more upstanding brothers. If he would not work, let him go hungry. It was a divine formulation. No less an authority on the heavenly scheme than Martin Luther could argue that "princes, lords, counsellors of state, and everybody should be prudent, and cautious in dealing with beggars, and learn that, whereas people will not give and help honest paupers and needy neighbors, as ordained by God, they give, by the persuasion of the devil, and contrary to God's judgment, ten times as much to Vagabonds and desperate rogues." Luther goes on to add a biographical note: "I have myself of late years been cheated and befooled by such tramps and liars more than I wish to confess."[24]

Twentieth-century thinking, as reflected in language, has moved the site of the vagrant's deficit from character or morals to personality or psychic apparatus. The "drunk" or "inebriate" has now become the "alcoholic." It is a *significant* change. Whereas the drunkard was a moral weakling, the alcoholic is a victim of forces outside his or her control. This change in viewpoint does not necessarily remove the stigma from the vagrant but it does shift the locus of responsibility for the affliction from character to psychic development or, perhaps, to genes. The inebriate chooses his or her debauchery; the alcoholic is a victim of his or her illness.

So, too, the "vagrant" has become the "homeless person." Vagrancy is a crime; homelessness is a condition of being without shelter. *On the surface* the new term appears to be more neutral, but, like the transition from "drunkard" to "alcoholic," the shift from "vagrant" to "homeless" tends to mask the opprobrium concealed within the new language. Homeless people, today, are still thought to be a rather unsavory lot; witness the recent comment of former president Reagan, who claimed that, given the availability of public shelters, the homeless obviously choose their unhappy living state. "They make it their own choice for staying out there," said Mr. Reagan, "There are shelters in virtually every city, and shelters here, and those people still prefer out there on the grates or the lawn to going into one of those shelters."[25]

Today's tendency to fractionate the homeless population into categories and subcategories is a more insidious process of masking opprobrium. It is argued, for example, that large numbers of today's homeless are people displaced from mental hospitals. In a sense, then, these products of deinstitutionalization are not truly homeless; they are mentally ill people who, because of wrong-headed judicial decisions and bad public policy, have been mistakenly put where they don't belong. Thus, if the mentally ill were returned to the institutions where they really belong, a significant portion of the homeless population would disappear.

It is true, we have seen, that the homeless population includes mentally ill people. What is not clear is how different this proportion is now as compared with earlier times or, indeed, whether it is any larger than that for the population as a whole. Since the advent of modern psychiatry the definition of mental illness has

broadened considerably. While once the term *lunacy* was reserved
for the more extreme instances of psychosis, mental illness now
embraces many variants of psychotic and neurotic behavior.
Mental illness, according to an ever-expanding definition, is quite
common in American society; some experts estimate that as much
as 25 percent of the *public at large* in urban areas suffers from
some form of mental illness. Given the expansiveness of modern
definitions of mental illness, it is not at all surprising that the
condition is prevalent among the homeless. And it is also certainly
true that the advent of psychotropic medications and the move
toward community mental health care had the effect of turning
large numbers of once hospitalized people out into the streets
with no adequate provision for their care and well-being.

But the emphasis on mental illness as an important feature
of homelessness has compounded the disgrace associated with
homeless life. The mentally ill suffer from a stigma of their own;
when it is accompanied by homelessness, the stigma of that
wretched status is enhanced. More importantly, people who emphasize mental illness as a significant feature of homelessness
shift the focus of public attention away from such troubling matters as serious flaws in our economic system and critical weak-
nesses in our social support system, and moves it to the more
restricted problems of mental illness and mental health. Many
members of the establishment would much prefer to ignore a
basic structural flaw in our socioeconomic system, whose correction would require a rethinking and reconstruction of the American system, and shift the blame for homelessness to the much
smaller arena of mental health and care for the mentally ill.

The same mechanism is at work when another segment of
the homeless population, the alcoholic and the drug addict, is
singled out for special attention. Substance abuse, as we have
seen, has always been found among the vagrant. Whether it was
or is more prevalent among the vagrant than it was or is among
the rooted citizens is doubtful. Alcohol and drug usage among
the homeless today may not be any more rampant than it is
among the general population. But, again, the attribution of such
addictions to the homeless tends to *medicalize* a phenomenon that
is primarily related to wages and the cost of shelter.

In essence, the transformation of the root cause of a social
problem from moral deficiency to illness changes the oppro-

brium attached to the problem only in form. To be a victim does not necessarily relieve the individual from the burden of stigma. The leper was always recognized as a victim; this recognition did not prevent society from driving the lepers from its midst. The alcoholic may be a victim, but he or she is still a drunk; the drug addict may be a victim, but he or she still remains a junkie. And if he or she is addicted to drink or drugs and also black, the stigma is further magnified.

If current homelessness is a contemporary incarnation of an old historical phenomenon, then its causes can be found in the risks attendant on the wage labor system. To shift attention from the economic system as the root cause of homelessness and to become preoccupied with homelessness as a problem in public health is to commit a historical error. Very few authorities, over the centuries, wanted to concede that the vagabonds that swarmed over the land were the victims of the economic system. After all, authorities wouldn't be authorities if they didn't have a strong stake in things as they are. It was always more convenient to construe the problem in terms of the deficiencies of individual human beings. These deficiencies were once attributed to moral flaws; today they are assigned to medical flaws. The common-sense notions that homeless people are poor and that they need wages to purchase food and shelter have been ignored.

Finally, we must deal in numbers because they are important. A social problem usually does not become a matter for serious public concern unless the numbers of people involved are substantial. Sometimes, however, problems emerge as foci for wide concern as a result of other factors—this is especially so today when an energetic and influential media can exaggerate an issue beyond all proportion. Moreover, the contemporary ethos allows for the rapid creation of interest groups and political constituencies that can agitate and command the attention of the same sensation-seeking media. The ordering of social problems into a hierarchy of importance has become a confusing and hazardous business. But for serious consideration of any contemporary social problem, it is essential that some reasonably accurate estimate of its magnitude be obtained.

Thus, we must count the homeless. It is a horrendous chore. Vagrancy by its very nature does not lend itself to enumeration. The vagrant does not appear on tax rolls or voting registers;

does not get counted by the census taker; and will be found, only occasionally, in the shelters, doss houses, and flophouses of the cities. He or she sleeps in caves, under trees and shrubs, in parks, on benches, in gullies and storm drains, on beaches, in doorways, in abandoned structures, in subways and bus stations, over and under heating grates, in utility conduits, and in a variety of other places probably known only to himself or herself and his or her homeless colleagues. Today, he or she may use an automobile, truck, or camper to provide protection from the elements. The vagrant may crash for a night or two with a friend, a relative, or even a stranger. He or she may be in jail, indistinguishable from the other criminals; in a mental hospital or a general medical hospital; in a cheap hotel; in a welfare-supported hotel; in a shelter or armory. He or she may be without a roof today and sheltered tomorrow and facing the elements again the following day. He or she will be in one place in winter, and another in summer.

The vagrant's existence becomes a nightmare for the quantitatively inclined social scientist. The paradox of the vagrant is that he or she is both visible and invisible at the same time. His or her presence is inescapable to the pedestrian who is approached for a handout or who nearly stumbles over the sleeping body, but the vagrant is invisible to the enumerator who must find that larger group that is hidden away, out of sight of police and other busybodies. And, when the vagrant is in jail or the hospital or a hotel, he or she is indistinguishable from the other inmates, patients, or guests. Indeed, when the vagrant is in a flophouse or a jail is he/she in fact homeless?

The definitional problem is critical, but it is also arbitrary. If the enumerator has a stake in finding large numbers, as in the case of an advocate for the homeless, he or she will find such numbers; if the enumerator is working for politicians who believe that the homeless population has been exaggerated by its advocates, he or she is likely to produce a smaller list. The homeless advocate may use a broader definition, or may search more diligently and produce higher numbers. Bias may lead him or her to count questionable cases in the homeless column, or he or she might deliberately exaggerate results. And the person who believes that the homeless problem is not all that serious may reverse any or all of these procedures, and thereby produce the smaller numbers that answer his or her own expectations. The dispassionate and objective census taker is a historical exception, but even he must draw a line.

Whatever the boundaries, however, the count is—for all the reasons mentioned above—difficult. Exactitude is out of the question. The best that can be done is to provide gross estimates with upper and lower limits. Prior to the nineteenth century, inventories of the homeless were almost nonexistent. The numbers of vagrants in those early days were provided by the agents of the Crown whose only stake in exaggeration was to justify their own terror of an unstable population and, at times, a very real need to siphon off the jail population so as to make room for more. Beginning with mid-nineteenth-century social awareness, however, the counts begin to take on a more compelling nature.

Henry Mayhew was meticulous but conservative. He followed a straightforward method: he counted the people in the tramp houses, workhouses, and jails of England, relying on the careful accounts kept by their managers and wardens. Thus, in 1839 some 115,000 different vagrants were counted in the tramp houses and other Poor Law shelters of England. This number increased considerably by the following decade: 310,058 were found in the metropolitan districts alone in the year 1848. The number dropped precipitously the following year, to 143,064 in the same districts. That the 1848 figure was in part a function of the great Irish exodus can be deduced from the data reported by the township of Warrington, which reported a total of 17,322 vagrants in its tramp houses of whom—it was carefully noted—12,038 were Irish. Warrington, evidently, was especially attuned to the perfidious Irish beggar.[26]

These data do not begin to address the question of those who did not come to the attention of Poor Law officials or the police. Those additional numbers are anybody's guess. By the middle of the nineteenth century, England was full of vagrants. Even being very conservative, and disregarding the existence of the uncounted, we end up with at least 200,000 wandering souls out of a population of approximately 17,000,000 people then residing in England and Wales. This comes to one in eighty-five

of *all* people, a group that includes, of course, women and in-
fants. The proportion of vagrants to adult males must have been
large indeed. And the Industrial Revolution, with its concomitant
upheaval, had not yet generated a full head of steam.

But Mayhew and his passion for detail aside, counting the
vagrant relied on the registers of the tramp houses. It was the
same strategy employed by American investigators as they grap-
pled with the hobo problem. Alice Solenberger, another of the
more sensible social scientists, reported that the Chicago Health
Department—based on its survey of municipal lodging houses
in 1907—estimated some 79,411 homeless. She preferred a
slightly more conservative figure: "a careful study of local conditions during the winter of 1907–08, estimated the number of
homeless men then in Chicago to be probably not less than
60,000."[27] Nels Anderson, writing in 1923, allows for an important seasonal variation: "In Chicago, all estimates are in substantial agreement that the population of Hobohemia never falls
below 30,000 in summer, doubles this figure in winter, and has
reached 75,000 and over in periods of unemployment."[28] The
seasonal change is, at first glance, counterintuitive. One would
think that the reasonable man would get out of Chicago in the
deep winter months and head for a warmer climate. We must,
however, remember that Chicago was the source of news about
and recruitment for work; during the off-seasons, the migratory
worker returned to that city. It was, so to speak, his home base.

Anderson's and Solenberger's counts are surprisingly similar
to that of Mayhew. Out of a Chicago population of some
3,000,000, the homeless comprised between 1 and 2 percent of
the total—almost exactly that of metropolitan England in the
mid–nineteenth century. That proportion seems to have changed,
though, with the coming of the Great Depression.

The enumeration method by then had not gotten more sophisticated, but there were additional sources of record keeping.
Lodging houses and shelters of various kinds did exist and they
provide some data. But the railroad companies had a particular
stake in the vagrant. He rode their trains without bothering to
buy a fare and, in the process, the hobo and tramp did not
hesitate to pilfer among the freight that was carried. Railroad

statistics, kept by angry officials, are a fascinating source of information. And the numbers are stupefying.

Grace Abbott, testifying before the Senate Committee that was considering the bill that eventually established the United States Transients Bureau, reported on the data she had collected from the various railroads. Mr. D. O'Connell, chief special agent of the Southern Pacific, wrote to her as follows:

> In response to your request, following are figures showing trespassers ejected from our trains and property:
>
> 1927 78,099
> 1928 89,568
> 1929 79,215
> 1930 170,641
> 1931 514,013
> 1932 ....683,457[29]

Mr. O'Connell's letter is horrifying testimony to the chaos wrought by the economic cataclysm of the 1930s. Over six hundred thousand people were kicked off the trains of *one* railroad in *one* year. He goes on to add that "the figures of ejectment tell only part of the story, as there were many trespassers whom it was impossible for our men to interfere with. The figures I have shown you, however, indicate very clearly the growth of this problem." They do indeed. He should have noted, though, that many of those "ejected" were repeaters; the hobo was a persistent creature. After being chased off one freight, he more than likely caught the next one to come along—possibly to be ejected once again.

The Southern Pacific was a major carrier and it went west. So did the smaller Western Pacific, which had some 928 miles of track running between Salt Lake City and San Francisco and which reported 64,132 ejections in the calendar year 1931. Many of these people undoubtedly went on to be chased off the Southern Pacific's roads. Nylander reports that 416,915 transients were "checked" on the Santa Fe in seven months of 1933.[30] Not all lines, however, kept such careful track of the ejecting activities of their private police forces. Some of them essentially gave up trying to control the problem of unticketed riders. A few tried to estimate the extent of the problem by using, as a base, the number of fatal accidents occurring on or about their trains. All that these numbers served to do was to show that the deaths and mutilations increased substantially during the early 1930s. The railroads of America had a special stake in seeing to it that something be done about the armies of people who trespassed on their properties, stole their goods, and damaged their equipment. The numbers are suspect, but to what extent?

The actual numbers of people made homeless by the depression will never be known: the U.S. Children's Bureau, at that time alert to the problems of youth, estimated that there were 200,000 boys roaming the countryside without home or shelter in 1932. *Fortune* magazine, not predisposed to overstate the case, claimed two million Americans were on the road in 1932.[31] The National Committee on the Care of the Transient and Homeless found 370,000 actually registered in hostels during three days in early 1933; the numbers of those without homes or wandering was placed at 1,250,000 or 1,500,000. That number is a far cry from the 500,000 boys alone claimed by frenzied advocates for the well-being of child vagrants. Considering the elusiveness of the population, the committee's figures are too low, and surely the 500,000 boys is much too high. But what are we to make of Mr. O'Connell's data? Perhaps it is enough to say that there were large numbers of people on the move during the depression and, like their historic counterparts, most of them were young and all were poor. Whatever the exact number, the problem was important and it was immense.

The homeless of the 1980s are no easier to count than those of earlier times. And as in other times, there are some who wish to find enormous numbers and others who prefer a lower figure. We have learned something about counting, however, in recent decades; inventories found today are more likely to be careful in their technique and assumptions. They all acknowledge the tremendous difficulties in arriving at good estimates of the number of homeless. Nonetheless, the estimates cover a wide range. A frequently quoted number comes from the Community for Creative Non-Violence: "two to three millions in the United States" (1986). This figure should be juxtaposed with the figure from a report of a task force from the Department of Housing and

Urban Development (1984) that argues for a range of between 192,000 to 586,000 homeless people.[32] The differences are a function of different enumeration strategies.

One of the more careful and responsible studies was conducted by Peter Rossi on the homeless in Chicago. His survey, fastidious and responsible, counted people in shelters, on the streets, and in doorways, bus stations, cars, hallways, and the like. The survey was conducted at two different times: in the fall of 1985 and the spring of 1986. Much to the chagrin of advocates for the homeless, Rossi found only two or three thousand homeless people in his search. His study has been criticized on various grounds, particularly his failure to include children—who, as we know, given the large number of poor, female-headed households, are prone to be among the homeless.[33]

Rossi tried to estimate the numbers of people who were homeless not only during a particular moment in time, but those who might have been in that condition over a more protracted period. He found that the homeless in Chicago probably numbered not more than five thousand different people for any given recent year. These numbers are a far cry from the Chicago of Alice Solenberger's time. But Chicago was a very different city in 1986. The hobo was long gone and the migratory laborer had no need to return to that metropolis to find another round of work. What is left in Chicago are the more recalcitrant vagrants—those who, as Rossi shows, are plagued by drink and without the wherewithal to pick up and move to warmer climates. But as he reminds the reader, Chicago's homeless are painfully poor.

The economic and housing problems facing the poor of the 1990s are very different from those that existed during the Great Depression and, indeed, those that faced other earlier generations of impoverished. There *does* exist, today, an elaborate welfare apparatus that provides some safety net for people facing economic disaster, especially children, mothers, the aged, and the disabled. The edifice of welfare programs that has evolved since the depression is weakest, however, for that population of people that has traditionally been most at risk for homelessness: the adult, unattached, and apparently able-bodied male who does not currently fit into any of the conventional categorical assistance programs.

The homeless today are not very much different from those of yesteryear. In spite of all their problems, which include physical and mental illness, alcoholism, and a lack of employment skills, the homeless person has an attachment to the labor market. Almost 40 percent of Rossi's respondents had worked in some capacity or another during the month prior to the survey. Indeed, one out of every four had had some gainful employment the very week they were counted as homeless. And his census focused on the dregs of Chicago's homeless—if that characterization can be allowed. Of course, much of this work was marginal—part-time, unskilled, and offering very little in the way of wages. But such work has always been the hallmark of the homeless.

When the need for that kind of employment begins to dwindle and when the secondary labor force becomes more isolated from the mainstream of labor, the problems of the homeless become acute. The homeless are on the extreme edge of the labor force. They have little in the way of occupational skills and they have a dearth of those personal characteristics that lead to success in a competitive job search. When times are good and the need for labor is great, the homeless have little trouble making ends meet—a little work here, a little there, with long spells of more consistent employment and shorter spells of nothing in between. In such times, their numbers diminish.

But when times are bad, as they are now for such marginally affiliated people, numbers of homeless increase. Their deficits become an obstacle; a tenuous psychological state, their substance abuse, and their erratic commitment to convention make it difficult to find work and to hold jobs. It is at such times that the deficit and disrepute of the homeless command the attention of the public at large. Their stigma rises to the fore, overshadowing their ordinary humanity. They become "ill" and a target for the new moralists of the civilization, the healers.

But it is more reasonable to focus on the labor market and on the utter catastrophe that afflicts the vast ghettos of our cities. Today's homeless need good jobs that pay decent wages. The homeless will work if they can find work. And they will persist in working if the material rewards warrant persistence.

Perhaps there is no better way to close than to quote again from that insightful highwayman of the sixteenth century who wrote to his king, a man who deeply believed that vagrancy was an act of willful malice: "for tell the begging Souldier, and the wandering and sturdy Beggar, that they are able to work for their living, and bid them go to work they will presently answer you, they would work if they could get it." King James didn't believe his correspondent, nor does it seem that public officials today are willing to accept so clear and intelligent a solution to the homeless problem.

Notes

Introduction

1. From Walt Whitman's "Song of the Open Road," in *Leaves of Grass* (New York: University Press, 1965).
2. There are exceptions: Nels Anderson is the most striking and his book, *The Hobo* (Chicago: University of Chicago Press, 1923), deserves its status as a classic. See also, Alice Solenberger, *One Thousand Homeless Men* (New York: Russell Sage Foundation, 1911), for a no-nonsense, dispassionate account.
3. The best known of such modern accounts is, perhaps, Josiah Flynt, *My Life* (New York: Outing Publishing, 1908). Also see Ben L. Reitman, ed., *Sister of the Road: The Autobiography of Box-Car Bertha* (New York: Harper and Row, 1937).
4. Phillip O'Connor, *Britain in the Sixties: Vagrancy* (Baltimore: Penguin Books, 1963), 20.
5. Henry Mayhew, *London Labour and the London Poor*, 4 vols. (1861–62; reprint, New York: Dover Publications, 1968).
6. Part of an anonymous verse, as quoted in Anderson, *The Hobo*, 202. It was written, apparently, during the time when the I.W.W. had made quite an impact on the hobo movement. The place of that rather remarkable radical movement in respect to hobo life is discussed more fully in chapter 2.
7. See chapter 1 for a more detailed discussion on these estimates and their sources.
8. Alexander Vexliard, *Introduction a la sociologie du vagabondage* (Paris: Librarie M. Riviere, 1956).

Chapter 1

1. In later times, when vagrants became subject to draconian penalties, begging students were given special letters of exemption from the punishments

of the law. Needless to say, some of the more enterprising "sturdy beggars" forged such licenses for themselves and others.

2. G. M. Trevelyan, *History of England,* 3 vols. (London: Longmans, Green and Company, 1934), 1:311–12.

3. Giovanni Boccaccio, *The Decameron* (Middlesex, England: Penguin Books, 1972), 50–58.

4. Phillip Ziegler, *The Black Death* (Middlesex, England: Penguin Books, 1969), 238. Ziegler is here referring to England. As to whether the same proportion would hold for the rest of Europe, Ziegler concludes "there is no obvious reason why it should not" (239). Historians with a demographic inclination have displayed a macabre interest in trying to arrive at mortality rates. Some authorities have generated estimates as high as 50 or 60 percent (Trevelyan).

5. Trevelyan, *History of England,* 1:313.

6. The ordinance was prepared in 1349, but since Parliament did not meet that year, probably because of the plague, the act was not formally proclaimed until 1351.

7. As cited in C. J. Ribton-Turner, *A History of Vagrants and Vagrancy* (Montclair, N.J.: Patterson Smith, 1972), 43–44.

8. The able-bodied are spoken of as "valient beggars" in the text of the statute; after some time they will be referred to as "sturdy beggars," and later still, as a subclass of the "unworthy poor."

9. Ziegler, *Black Death,* 247.

10. Trevelyan, *History of England,* 1:318.

11. Ibid., 1:320.

12. The discovery of the ocean routes and subsequent trade with England's new colonies gave London a very special maritime character.

13. Trevelyan, *History of England,* 2:31. Enclosure was not without its critics, however, nor did it occur without attempts at legislative control. Recognizing how disruptive enclosure could be, the government on numerous occasions tried to slow the process down. The lure of wealth, however, prevailed.

14. Ribton-Turner, *Vagrants and Vagrancy,* 90.

15. Ribton-Turner, *Vagrants and Vagrancy* (my emphasis), 90.

16. Ibid. When not paraphrasing, I have changed the language of the ordinance from its older form of English to make it more readable.

17. Samuel E. Wallace, *Skid Row as a Way of Life* (Totowa, N. J.: Bedminster Press, 1965), 5–6.

18. As quoted by Ribton-Turner, *Vagrants and Vagrancy,* 139 (my emphasis).

19. A folk rhyme of the times, as quoted by Christopher Hill, in *The Century of Revolution: 1603–1714* (Edinburgh: Thomas Nelson and Sons, 1961), 129.

20. A. L. Beier, *Masterless Men: The Vagrancy Problem in England 1560–1640* (London: Methuen, 1985), 162.

21. See Ribton-Turner, *Vagrants and Vagrancy,* 143–44, for a series of letters between King James and Sir Thomas Smyth of Virginia in part concerned with the lack of boats.

22. Ribton-Turner, *Vagrants and Vagrancy*, 154.

23. Beier, *Masterless Men*, 56.

24. The notion of the masterless man is best captured in Beier's unique attempt to portray the dispossessed of this English era, *Masterless Men*.

25. Beier, *Masterless Men*, 87.

26. Ibid., 89.

27. The American hobo had its mythical kings: Jeff Davis, of the Hobos of America, Inc. and James Eads How, the "millionaire tramp" and self-anointed king. Such folk had a grand time hoodwinking romantics and gullible journalists. See Nels Anderson, *Men on the Move* (Chicago: University of Chicago Press, 1940), for more about these characters.

28. Beier, *Masterless Men*, 89.

29. Ibid., 90.

30. Ibid., 174.

31. Steven Marcus, *Engels, Manchester, and the Working Class* (New York: Vintage Books, 1974), 7.

32. John A. Garraty, *Unemployment in History* (New York: Harper and Row, 1978).

33. Charles Dickens, *Hard Times* (Oxford: Oxford University Press, 1989), 147.

34. Marcus, *Engels, Manchester, and the Working Class*, 184–85.

35. Jacob A. Riis, *How the Other Half Lives* (1890; reprint, New York: Hill and Wang, 1957).

36. For a wrenching portrayal of the São Paulo *flavela*, see Carolina Maria de Jesus, *Child of the Dark* (New York: Signet, 1962).

37. Mayhew, *London Labor and the London Poor*, 4 vols. (1861–62; reprint, New York: Dover Publications, 1968), 3:368.

38. Marcus, *Engels, Manchester, and the Working Class*, 206.

39. As quoted in Beier, *Masterless Men*.

40. Gareth Stedman Jones, *Outcast London* (Oxford: Clarendon Press, 1971), 343.

41. David Matza and Henry Miller, "Poverty and Proletariat" in *Contemporary Social Problems*, 4th ed., ed. Robert K. Merton and Robert Nisbet (New York: Harcourt, Brace, Jovanovich, 1976).

42. There was a resurgence of the problem in Great Britain during the late 1960s, much like the one that was apparent in the United States at the same time. This was in part a function of that island's "hippie" phenomenon compounded by a swarm of runaway youth. See, for example, Noel Timms, *Rootless in the City* (London: Blackfriars Press, 1968) and the Home Office, *Report of the Working Party on Vagrancy and Street Offences* (London: Her Majesty's Stationery Office, 1976).

Chapter 2

1. Walter I. Trattner, *From Poor Law to Welfare State* (New York: Free Press, 1974).
2. From John Winthrop's *Journal,* quoted by Trattner, *From Poor Law to Welfare State,* 25.
3. For example, James P. Beckwourth, a significant figure in the American Fur Company, became a Crow war chief. Beckwourth had been, too, one of the few black trappers. See Bernard De Voto, *Across the Wide Missouri* (Boston: Houghton Mifflin, 1947).
4. De Voto, *Across the Wide Missouri,* 103.
5. See De Voto, *Across the Wide Missouri,* 103–4, for the details of these costs and wages.
6. Herbert Ashbury, *The Barbary Coast* (New York: Capricorn, 1933), 15.
7. Ibid., 120–21.
8. Rodman Wilson Paul, *Mining Frontiers of the Far West: 1848–1880* (New York: Holt, Rinehart and Winston, 1963), 15.
9. Ibid., 26. In 1860 the census reported some 34,933 Chinese out of a state population of 380,000 (*Mining Frontiers,* 35).
10. From a ditty of the times, quoted in Paul, *Mining Frontiers,* 26.
11. Paul, *Mining Frontiers,* 37–38.
12. Thomas Cochran and William Miller, *The Age of Enterprise* (New York: Harper and Row, 1961), 55.
13. Ibid., 131.
14. Edward Everett Dale, *Frontier Ways* (Westport, Conn.: Greenwood, 1959), 9.
15. Ibid., 15. Among these Europeans was the marquis de Mores, a French nobleman, and Baron von Richthofen, an ancestor of the famous flying ace of World War I.
16. From the memoirs of a cowboy, as quoted in David Dary, *Cowboy Culture* (New York: Alfred A. Knopf, 1981), 275.
17. Dary, *Cowboy Culture,* 282.
18. Ibid., 276.
19. Ibid., 291.
20. This cowboy song was still sung early in this century; see Dary, *Cowboy Culture,* 296.
21. Dary, *Cowboy Culture,* 298.
22. Ibid., 302.
23. Nels Anderson, *The Hobo* (Chicago: University of Chicago Press, 1923), 162–63.
24. As quoted in Anderson, *The Hobo,* 161.
25. Anderson, *The Hobo,* 160.
26. As cited by Anderson, *The Hobo,* 194–95.
27. From the preamble to the constitution of the I.W.W., as quoted in Anderson, *The Hobo,* 233.

28. Kenneth Allsop, *Hard Travellin': The Hobo and His History* (New York: New American Library, 1967), 126.
29. Ibid., 126.
30. Sung to the tune of "Tipperary"; see Anderson, *The Hobo*, 208.
31. These costs are derived from Anderson and reflect prices that existed around the year 1920.
32. Anderson, *The Hobo*, 34.
33. Part of a song written by Joe Hill; see Anderson, *The Hobo*, 210.
34. These counts are derived from the crude sketch of that West Madison St. block found in Anderson, *The Hobo*, 15.
35. Anderson, *The Hobo*, xxi.
36. Howard M. Bahr, *Skid Row: An Introduction to Disaffiliation* (New York: Oxford University Press, 1973), 32.
37. Samuel E. Wallace, *Skid Row as a Way of Life* (Totowa, N.J.: Bedminster Press, 1965).
38. Bahr, *Disaffiliated Man: Essays and Bibliography on Skid Row, Vagrancy, and Outsiders* (Toronto: University of Toronto) 1970, 103.

Chapter 3

1. *New York Times*, 25 October 1929. Copyright © 1929/1932 by The New York Times Company. Reprinted by permission.
2. David A. Shannon, *The Great Depression* (Englewood Cliffs, N.J.: Prentice-Hall, 1960), 3.
3. Milton Meltzer, *Brother, Can You Spare a Dime?* (New York: Random House, 1973), 17.
4. Shannon, *Great Depression*, 5.
5. See, for example, Nathan Cohen, *Social Work in the American Tradition* (New York: Dryden Press, 1958), 161 ff.; and Joan Crouse, *The Homeless Transient in the Great Depression: New York State, 1929–1941* (Albany: State University of New York, 1986).
6. Cohen, *Social Work*, 162.
7. Garraty, *Unemployment in History*, 167.
8. Shannon, *Great Depression*, 7.
9. Ibid., 7.
10. Ibid., 11.
11. As quoted in Studs Terkel, *Hard Times* (New York: Random House, 1970), 20.
12. Crouse, *Homeless Transient*, 48.
13. Ibid., 52.
14. Ibid., 101.
15. James Rorty, "Counting the Homeless," *Nation*, 21 June 1933.
16. A. Wayne McMillen, "Migrant Boys," *Social Service Review* 7, no. 1 (March 1933): 64–83.
17. Towne Nylander, "Wandering Youth," *Sociology and Social Research*, 17, no. 6 (1933): 560–68.

18. David M. Schneider, "Transient Youth in This Century and the Last," *Jewish Social Service Quarterly* 9, no. 3 (June 1933): 305–9.

19. Meltzer, *Brother, Can You Spare a Dime?* 49–50.

20. Thomas Minehan, *Boy and Girl Tramps of America* (New York: Farrar and Rinehart, 1934). In spite of its title, Minehan has very little to say about girl tramps.

21. Crouse, *Homeless Transient*, 126.

22. *New York Times,* 7 October 1932. Copyright © 1929/1932 by The New York Times Company. Reprinted by permission.

23. Gertrude Springer, as quoted in Crouse, *Homeless Transient*, 131.

24. The case of John McClosky, discussed in Nels Anderson, *Men on the Move* (Chicago: University of Chicago Press, 1940), 74.

25. Anderson, *Men on the Move*, 76.

26. J. N. Webb, *The Transient Unemployed*, Works Progress Administration Research Monograph no. 3 (Washington, D.C.: U.S. Government Printing Office, 1938), 130.

27. Crouse, *Homeless Transient*, 106.

28. As quoted in Crouse, *Homeless Transient*, 107.

29. Meltzer, *Brother, Can You Spare a Dime?* 79–80.

30. Webb, *Transient Unemployed*, 101.

31. John N. Webb and Malcolm Brown, *Migrant Families*, Works Progress Administration Research Monograph no. 18 (Washington, D.C.: U.S. Government Printing Office, 1935), xiv.

32. Data are from Anderson, *Men on the Move*, 99–132.

33. Webb and Brown, *Migrant Families*, 22.

34. Ibid., 23.

35. Shannon, *Great Depression*, 25.

36. Terkel, *Hard Times*, 214.

37. Garraty, *Unemployment in History*, 178.

38. As quoted in Garraty, *Unemployment in History*, 179. Paul Lazarsfeld's book, *Marienthal*, has not been published in English. See Garraty, 173, note 10.

39. Garraty, *Unemployment in History*, 181.

40. Ibid.

41. Crouse, *Homeless Transient*, 195.

42. Harry Hopkins, *Spending to Save* (New York: W. W. Norton, 1936), 127–28.

Chapter 4

1. Much of what follows in this chapter derives from a study conducted in the Haight-Ashbury district of San Francisco during the years 1967–71. The project was supported in part by the National Institute of Mental Health, Grant MH 1537, and was directed by Dr. Stephen Pittel. It was, as far as I can determine, the only longitudinal investigation of the young

people in that neighborhood who might have styled themselves as hippies. The results of that unique inquiry can be found in various publications of the project staff. The most comprehensive account of the findings can be found in an unpublished monograph, *Dropping Down*, by Stephen Pittel and Henry Miller. The contribution of Dr. Pittel to the ideas and data in this chapter is gratefully acknowledged.

2. Nathan Adler deserves credit for placing the hippie experience in the context of a larger Western history. See his *The Underground Stream: New Life-Styles and the Antinomian Personality* (New York: Harper and Row, 1972). The similarity between the hippies and more traditional bohemians has been well argued by Bennet Berger, "Hippie Morality—More Old than New," *Transaction* 5, no. 2 (December 1967), 19–27.

3. Nathan Adler, *Underground Stream*, 27. Copyright © 1972 by Nathan Adler. Reprinted by permission of Harper Collins Publishers.

4. Adler, *Underground Stream*, 29.

5. Norman Cohn, *The Pursuit of the Millennium* (New York: Oxford University Press, 1970), 159.

6. From a contemporary critique of the Ranters as quoted in Cohn, *Millennium*, 291.

7. From another critic quoted in Cohn, *Millennium*, 292.

8. Yet another exegesis of Ranter belief from Cohn, *Millennium*, 293.

9. Cohn, *Millennium*, 301.

10. Adler, *Underground Stream*, 38.

11. Ibid., 45.

12. The opera was based on that most influential document of bohemian history, Henry Murger's *Scenes of Bohemian Life*.

13. Adapted from Berger, "Hippie Morality," 19–20. Berger, in turn, derived these canons of bohemianism from Malcolm Cowley's *Exile's Return: A Literary Odyssey of the 1920s* (New York: Viking Press, 1951).

14. Howard Becker, *German Youth* (New York: Oxford University Press, 1946), 67.

15. Adler, *Underground Stream*, 46–47.

16. Ibid., 47.

17. This and the following two case extractions are from Pittel and Miller, *Dropping Down*. They represent excerpts from some of the case studies of over two hundred hippies interviewed in 1968 by the Haight-Ashbury Research Project. The study followed a group of young men and women who had lived in the area during 1967–68 for the next two years of their lives. As might be guessed, the majority of them drifted back into conventional life. Although the data could not speak to what became of them after the early 1970s, it is not unreasonable to think that many went on to become today's yuppies.

18. The Hell's Angels, at that time, under the prompting of their leader, Sonny Barger, offered the services of the club to Lyndon Johnson to go to Vietnam as a special unit and put a quick end to the war. The offer went unacknowledged.

19. The following three vignettes are taken from Pittel and Miller, *Dropping Down*.

20. Charles Perry, *The Haight-Ashbury* (New York: Random House, 1984), 125–26. Copyright © 1984 by Charles Perry. Reprinted by permission of Random House Inc.

21. Perry, *Haight-Ashbury*, 127.

22. Some of the "old time" hippies would lament that the only people left to be found on the streets of the Haight-Ashbury were journalists, television cameramen, tourists, academic researchers, and narcotics agents.

23. Perry, *Haight-Ashbury*, 171.

24. Ibid., 181.

25. *San Francisco Chronicle*, 24 March 1967.

26. Helen Swick Perry, *The Human Be-In* (New York: Basic Books, 1970), 23.

27. Perry, *Human Be-In*, 23.

28. One-half of the subjects involved in the Haight-Ashbury Research Project had come to San Francisco to participate in the 1967 "summer of love." On average, they had been in the city for slightly less than one year and had lived in a median of six different residences. Ninety percent of the subjects were single; sixty-five percent had no regular sexual partner. Seventy-five percent were living with other people, mostly as "roommates" or in communes. Six percent had absolutely no place of residence, and lived on the streets or in parks.

29. Perry, *Haight-Ashbury*, 97.

30. Living expenses for the Haight study subjects averaged $175 a month, which they managed to raise from a variety of different sources. Slightly more than 20 percent of them received at least some money from parents, 30 percent worked at part-time jobs (mostly as unskilled laborers, or in clerical or sales positions), and 20 percent were on public assistance. Over half earned at least some money from dealing drugs. Other sources of income, aside from panhandling, included modeling and acting, and sometimes baby-sitting.

31. In San Francisco, the total number of narcotic arrests increased from 1,100 in 1963 to 4,096 in 1967. The arrest rate continued to climb moderately until 1967 when an 85 percent jump was recorded. The contribution of Haight-Ashbury to these figures was estimated by the city police department as about 39 percent of the total. The most dramatic shift was in regard to the increase in juvenile arrests for narcotics violations: from nine in 1963 to 446 in 1967 with a yearly increment averaging well over 150 percent (Stephen Pittel, "The Current Status of the Haight-Ashbury Hippie Community," unpublished manuscript, 1968).

32. The median annual income of the Haight study subjects' families was between $13,000 and $15,000. Almost 90 percent of the subjects' fathers were employed as executives and professionals (24 percent), administrators and managers (24 percent), clerks (20 percent), or skilled laborers (20 percent). Ten percent of these fathers were employed as semiskilled or unskilled laborers. Both fathers and mothers had had a median of one

year of college education. Almost 30 percent of the fathers and 15 percent of the mothers were college graduates; 15 percent of fathers and 7 percent of mothers had higher degrees.

33. Perry, *Haight-Ashbury*, 244.
34. The diversity and extent of drug use among the study subjects was quite remarkable: on the average some thirteen different psychoactive drugs had been used or experimented with; 25 percent of the sample had used between eighteen and twenty-nine different drugs. The average number of psychedelic "trips" for a subject was between seventy-five and one hundred experiences. Some subjects reported over three hundred "trips."
35. See, especially, Kenneth Kenniston, *The Uncommitted* (New York: Harcourt, Brace, and World, 1965), whose entire book is concerned with these matters.
36. Slightly more than 25 percent of the subjects in the Haight-Ashbury research study had been arrested for the use or sale of drugs.

Chapter 5

1. Julia Vinograd, "Downhill," *Berkeley Street Cannibals* (Berkeley, Calif.: Oyez, 1976).
2. Much of the material found in this chapter derives from a study of the street people of Berkeley, California, conducted in the spring of 1973. Dr. James Baumohl, currently of McGill University and at that time a graduate student in the School of Social Welfare, University of California, Berkeley, conceived the idea of a systematic census of the many scores of hungry young people who gathered each afternoon at the Berkeley Emergency Food Project. The idea was to gather reliable data on a population of youth who presented a most perplexing problem not only to Berkeley but to many other communities across the nation. The results of that study can be found in Jim Baumohl and Henry Miller, *Down and Out in Berkeley* (City of Berkeley-University of California Community Affairs Committee, 1974). That monograph, in essence, was our final report to the university-city committee that had been good enough to provide modest funding for the inquiry. For a good deal of what follows, I owe heartfelt thanks to Jim Baumohl and that committee.
3. For a fascinating account of how the habitué of the streets in the immediate posthippie era achieved his sobriquet, see Robert Kapsis and Robert Michels, "The Street People: A Case Study of Rumor Formation" (University of California, Berkeley, June 1970, mimeographed pamphlet).
4. Sondra J. Betsch, "Penny Economy" (Paper presented at the annual meeting of the Society for the Study of Social Problems, 27 August 1973), New York.
5. Jerry Rubin, *Do It! Scenarios of the Revolution* (New York: Simon and Schuster, 1970), 24.

6. Betsch, "Penny Economy."

7. Abraham Miller, "On the Road: Hitchhiking on the Highway," *Society*, July–August 1973, 14.

8. The ad hoc social agency of the time is a phenomenon worthy of a study in itself. The wide variety of such organizations included improvised shelters; runaway centers; free medical clinics manned by volunteer physicians and nurses; rap centers; switchboards and hot lines; drug testing services; food kitchens; free "universities"; and many others. The life history of organizations such as these has been described in Henry Miller and Connie Philipp, "The Alternative Service Agency," *Handbook of Clinical Social Work*, in Aaron Rosenblatt and Diana Waldfogel (eds.) (San Francisco: Jossey-Bass, 1983).

9. U.S. Department of Commerce, Bureau of the Census, *Statistical Abstract of the United States, 1988*, 125.

10. As expected, there was some difference between blacks and whites regarding geographic origin. Blacks tended more frequently to have been born in southern states (36.6 percent as opposed to 14.9 percent) and in large cities (70 percent as opposed to 54 percent). Additionally, no blacks in this study were born or raised in the Central Plains, the Mountain states, or in New England. Blacks, however, showed a higher percentage of Bay Area–born (16.7 percent versus 9.3 percent).

11. Specifically, a family was considered "itinerant" if it had moved to at least four different cities, spending no more than two continuous years in any one.

12. Of these thirty-four, two were full-time students and nine others were on welfare. Of those receiving welfare, most were women concerned about adequate care for their children, or individuals with psychiatric disabilities who felt that they could not work. For the sample as a whole, we found no difference between welfare recipients and others regarding the desire to work.

13. Comparable studies of street people in other communities had been accomplished during the early 1970s, perhaps with less detail. Their findings are, as we indicated, quite similar. See for example, "On the Streets of Isla Vista" Counseling Center, University of California, Santa Barbara, and the Isla Vista Switchboard, 1971(?); Robert Beall Burnside Projects, Inc., *A Survey of Persons Who Use Social Services on Skid Row* (Portland, Ore.: Author, 1973); Peter F. Mason, "Some Characteristics of a Youth Ghetto in Boulder, Colorado," *Journal of Geography* 71 (December 1972) 526–532; Travelers Aid Society, *Annual Statistical Report on Travelers Aid Services* (New York: Author, 1974 and 1975). Further, a large variety of reports, monographs, notes, and other such materials were devoted to runaways and "throwaways"—a problem that had raised a great deal of public concern during the 1970s.

14. For the idea of a youth ghetto, see John F. Lofland, "The Youth Ghetto: A Perspective on the 'Cities of Youth' Around Our Large Universities," *Journal of Higher Education* 39, no. 3 (March 1968) 121–143; and Peter F.

Mason, "Some Spatial and Locational Relationships Relevant to Youth Ghetto Disorder," *Proceedings of the Association of American Geographers*, 5 (1973), 165–169.

Chapter 6

1. Paul Kennedy, *The Rise and Fall of the Great Powers* (New York: Random House, 1987).
2. Much of these data, and those that follow, derive from the *Statistical Abstract of the United States*, U.S. Department of Commerce, Bureau of the Census. These abstracts are published annually and provide a rich encyclopedia of statistical data on all sorts of things. I used the abstracts for 1963, 1986, and 1988.
3. Michael Harrington, *The Other America: Poverty in the United States* (New York: Macmillan, 1962). This book served as an antidote to John Kenneth Galbraith's very popular treatment of the new economic miracle, *The Affluent Society* (Boston: Houghton Mifflin, 1958).
4. These estimates can be found in David M. Gordon, *Theories of Poverty and Underemployment* (Lexington, Mass.: D. C. Heath, 1972), 99. Gordon admits that more hopeful figures, generated by the Council of Economic Advisors, backcast a decline from 32 percent in 1947 to 21 percent in 1960. The differences result from a dearth of data as well as deficiencies in the definition of absolute poverty.
5. In 1960 the threshold was $3,022; by 1987 it had risen to $11,611. This is for an urban family of four people.
6. Matza and Miller, "Poverty and Proletariat," *Contemporary Social Problems*, R. K. Merton and R. Nisbet (eds.) (New York: Harcourt Brace Jovanovich, 1976) 639–673.
7. Leon H. Keyserling, *Progress or Poverty*, Conference on Economic Progress, Washington, D.C., 1964, 34.
8. Data on poverty rates are taken from Bureau of the Census, *Poverty in the U.S., 1987*, Current Population Reports, Consumer Income, Series P-160, no. 163, table 1. The rate for blacks, in the text, is for the year 1959.
9. Keyserling, *Progress or Poverty*, 39.
10. In 1974, when the economy began to sour, the poverty rate began to climb until it reached a level in 1983 of 15.2 percent. Since then it has descended, slowly, to 13.5 percent as of 1987; still a distance from the all-time low of 1973.
11. Gordon, *Theories of Poverty and Underemployment*, 6.
12. Ibid., 45.
13. Ibid., 47.
14. Michael S. Carliner, "Homelessness: A Housing Problem?" in *The Homeless in Contemporary Society*, ed. R. D. Bingham, Roy E. Green, and S. B. White (Newbury Park, Calif.: Sage, 1987), 120.

15. *Statistical Abstract of the United States,* 1988, table 739.
16. A very recent study by the Center on Budget and Policy Priorities (1989) makes the point even more emphatic. The shortage of housing for the poor is huge and growing: half of the nation's poor spend at least 70 percent of their income on housing. Further, as of 1985, there was a shortage of 3.7 million such units in 1970. Since 1985 the problem could only have gotten worse. (My source is the *San Francisco Chronicle,* 11 July, 1989.)
17. Carliner, *The Homeless,* 121.
18. Almost all studies of the contemporary homeless note the wide prevalence of alcohol abuse. Rates vary from inquiry to inquiry, but fall within a range of 25 to 40 percent of homeless males. For women, the estimates are much lower. It is worthwhile to note that these estimates are much like those Howard Bahr (see bibliography) presented in his studies of the old skid rows. For a summary of the research on alcohol use among the current homeless populations, see Committee on Health Care for Homeless People, *Homelessness, Health, and Human Needs* (Washington, D.C.: National Academy Press, 1988), chapter 3; and Mary E. Stefl, "The New Homeless," in *The Homeless in Contemporary Society,* ed. R. D. Bingham, Roy E. Green, and S. B. White (Newbury Park, Calif.: Sage, 1987).
19. Marjorie Robertson, "Homeless Veterans, an Emerging Problem" in *The Homeless in Contemporary Society,* ed. R. D. Bingham, Roy E. Green, and S. B. White (Newbury Park, Calif.: Sage, 1987).
20. These ranges derive from the Committee on Health Care for Homeless People, *Homelessness,* chapter 3, table 3–10.
21. See Committee on Health Care for Homeless People, Homelessness, chapter 3, especially table 3–7. Rossi, Fisher, and Willis's Chicago sample revealed that 22.4 percent admitted to at least one mental health hospitalization, a figure remarkably close to that of the Berkeley street people. (Peter Rossi, Gene A. Fisher, and Georgianna Willis, *The Condition of the Homeless of Chicago,* Report of the Social and Demographic Research Institute, University of Massachusetts, Amherst, and NORC, Social Science Research Center, University of Chicago.)
22. Mayhew, *London Labour and the London Poor,* 3:402.
23. See the Committee on Health Care for Homeless People, *Homelessness,* table 1–2. Rossi, Fisher, and Willis found that 35.5 percent of the Chicago homeless were black (*Condition of the Homeless,* 63).
24. J. C. Hotten, *Liber Vagatorum* (1592; reprint, London: Penguin Press, 1932).
25. "Reagan on Homelessness: Many Choose to Live in the Streets," *New York Times,* 23 December 1988.
26. These data derive from Mayhew, *London Labor,* 3:368 and following pages.
27. Alice Solenberger, *One Thousand Homeless Men* (New York: Russell Sage Foundation, 1911), 9.
28. Anderson, *The Hobo,* 13.
29. As quoted in A. Wayne McMillen, "Migrant Boys: Some Data from Salt Lake City," *Social Service Review,* 7, no. 1 (1933), 65.

30. Towne Nylander, "Wandering Youth," *Sociology and Social Research,* 17, no. 6 (1933): 56–68; "The Migrant Population of the United States," *American Journal of Sociology,* 30, no. 2 (1924): 129–53.
31. *Fortune,* February 1933, 46.
32. Office of Policy Development and Research, U.S. Department of Housing and Urban Development, *A Report to the Secretary on the Homeless and Emergency Shelters* (Washington, D.C.: U.S. Government Printing Office, 1984).
33. Rossi, Fisher, and Willis, *Condition of the Homeless,* 39–58.

Bibliography

Adler, Nathan. *The Underground Stream: New Life-Styles and the Antinomian Personality.* New York: Harper and Row, 1972.

Allsop, Kenneth. *Hard Travellin': The Hobo and His History.* New York: New American Library, 1970.

Anderson, Nels. *The Hobo: The Sociology of the Homeless Man.* Chicago: University of Chicago Press, 1923.

————. *Men on the Move.* Chicago: University of Chicago Press, 1940.

Ashbury, Herbert. *The Barbary Coast.* New York: Capricorn, 1933.

Bahr, Howard M. *Disaffiliated Man: Essays and Bibliography on Skid Row, Vagrancy, and Outsiders.* Toronto: University of Toronto, 1970.

————. *Skid Row: An Introduction to Disaffiliation.* New York: Oxford University Press, 1973.

Baumohl, J., and H. Miller. *Down and Out in Berkeley: An Overview of a Study of Street People.* Report prepared for the City of Berkeley-University of California Community Affairs Committee. Berkeley, Calif.: University of California Community Affairs Committee, 1974.

Becker, Howard. *German Youth.* New York: Oxford University Press, 1946.

Beier, A. L. *Masterless Men: The Vagrancy Problem in England 1560–1640.* London: Methuen, 1985.

Berger, Bennet. "Hippie Morality—More Old than New." *Transaction* 5, no. 2 (1967), 19–27.

Berger, B. M. *Looking for America: Essays on Youth, Suburbia, and Other American Obsessions.* Englewood Cliffs, N.J.: Prentice-Hall, 1971.

Betsch, Sondra J. "Penny Economy." Paper presented at the annual meeting of the Society for the Study of Social Problems, 27 August 1973, New York.

Blenkner, M., and J. M. Elder. "Migrant Boys in Wartime as Seen by U.S.O. Travelers Aid." *Social Service Review* 19 (September 1945): 324–42.

Boccaccio, G. *The Decameron.* Middlesex, England: Penguin Books, 1972.

Caplow, T. "Transiency as a Cultural Pattern." *American Sociological Review* 5 (October 1940): 731–739.

Carliner, Michael S. "Homelessness: A Housing Problem?" In *The Homeless in Contemporary Society*, edited by R. D. Bingham, R. E. Green, and S. B. White. Newbury Park, Calif.: Sage, 1987.

Chambliss, W. J. "The Law of Vagrancy." *Warner Modular Publications*, Module no. 4 (1973): 1–10.

Cochran, Thomas, and William Miller. *The Age of Enterprise*. New York: Harper and Row, 1961.

Cohen, Nathan. *Social Work in the American Tradition*. New York: Dryden Press, 1958.

Cohn, Norman. *The Pursuit of the Millenium*. New York: Oxford University Press, 1970.

Committee on Health Care for Homeless People. *Homelessness, Health, and Human Needs*. Washington, D.C.: National Academy Press, 1988.

Cowley, M. *Exile's Return: A Literary Odyssey of the 1920s*. New York: Viking Press, 1951.

Crouse, Joan M. *The Homeless Transient in the Great Depression: New York State, 1929–1941*. Albany: State University of New York Press, 1986.

Dale, Edward Everett. *Frontier Ways: Sketches of Life in the Old West*. Westport, Conn.: Greenwood Press, 1959.

Dary, David. *Cowboy Culture: A Saga of Five Centuries*. New York: Alfred A. Knopf, 1981.

de Jesus, Carolina Maria. *Child of the Dark*. New York: Signet, 1962.

De Voto, Bernardo. *Across the Wide Missouri*. Boston: Houghton Mifflin, 1947.

Dickens, C. *Hard Times*. Oxford: Oxford University Press, 1989.

First, R. J., D. Roth, and B. D. Arewa. "Homelessness: Understanding the Dimensions of the Problem for Minorities." *Social Work* 33, no. 2 (1988): 120–24.

Flynt, J. *My Life*. New York: Outing Publishing, 1908.

Galbraith, John Kenneth. *The Affluent Society*. Boston: Houghton Mifflin, 1958.

Garraty, John A. *Unemployment in History*. New York: Harper and Row, 1958.

Gist, N. P., and L. A. Halbert. *Urban Society*. New York: Thomas Y. Crowell, 1933.

Gordon, David M. *Theories of Poverty and Underemployment*. Lexington, Mass.: D. C. Heath, 1972.

Harrington, Michael. *The Other America: Poverty in the United States*. New York: Macmillan, 1962.

Herrmann, O. *Pirates and Piracy*. New York: Stettiner Brothers, 1902.

Hill, Christopher. *The Century of Revolution: 1603–1714*. Edinburgh: Thomas Nelson and Sons, 1961.

Hinckle, W. "A Social History of the Hippies." *Ramparts* 5, no. 9 (1976): 5–26.

Hope, M., and J. Young. *The Faces of Homelessness*. Lexington, Mass.: Lexington Books, 1986.

Hopkins, Harry. *Spending to Save*. New York: W. W. Norton, 1936.

Hotten, J. C. *Liber Vagatorum*. 1592. Reprint. London: Penguin Press, 1932.

Huggins, M. K. *From Slavery to Vagrancy in Brazil: Crime and Social Control in the New World*. New Brunswick, N. J.: Rutgers University Press, 1985.

Ignatieff, M. *The Needs of Strangers*. New York: Viking Penguin, 1986.

Institute of Medicine. *Homelessness, Health, and Human Needs*. Washington, D.C.: National Academy Press, 1988.

Jones, Gareth Stedman. *Outcast London: A Study in the Relationship between Classes in Victorian Society*. Oxford: Clarendon Press, 1971.

Kapsis, Robert, and Robert Michels. *The Street People: A Case Study of Rumor Formation*. (unpublished paper) University of California, Berkeley, June 1970.

Kennedy, Paul. *The Rise and Fall of the Great Powers*. New York: Random House, 1987.

Kenniston, Kenneth. *The Uncommitted: Alienated Youth in American Society*. New York: Harcourt, Brace, and World, 1965.

Keyserling, Leon H. *Progress or Poverty*. Conference on Economic Progress, Washington, D.C., 1964.

Komisar, L. *Down and Out in the USA: A History of Social Welfare*. New York: Franklin Watts, 1973.

Lofland, John F. "The Youth Ghetto: A Perspective on the 'Cities of Youth' Around Our Large Universities." *Journal of Higher Education* 39, no. 3 (March 1968): 121–143.

MacLeod, C. *Horatio Alger, Farewell: The End of the American Dream*. New York: Seaview Books, 1980.

McMillen, A. Wayne. "Migrant Boys: Some Data from Salt Lake City." *Social Service Review* 7, no. 1 (1933): 64–83.

Manchester, W. "Rock Bottom in America." *New York*, August 1974, 24–46.

Marcus, Stephen. *Engels, Manchester, and the Working Class*. New York: Vintage Books, 1974.

Mason, P. F. "Some Characteristics of a Youth Ghetto in Boulder, Colorado. *Journal of Geography* 71 (December 1972): 526–532.

———. "Some Spatial and Locational Relationships Relevant to Youth Ghetto Disorder." *Proceedings of the Association of American Geographers* 5 (1973), 165–169.

Matza, David, and Henry Miller. "Poverty and Proletariat." In *Contemporary Social Problems*, 4th ed., edited by R. K. Merton and R. Nisbet. New York: Harcourt Brace Jovanovich, 1976.

Mayhew, Henry. *London Labour and the London Poor*. 1861–62. Reprint. New York: Dover Publications, 1968.

Meltzer, Milton. *Brother, Can You Spare a Dime?: The Great Depression 1929–1933*. New York: Random House, 1973.

Miller, Abraham. "On the Road: Hitchhiking on the Highway." *Society*, July–August 1973.

Miller, Henry, and Connie Philipp. "The Alternative Service Agency." In *Handbook of Clinical Social Work*, edited by Aaron Rosenblatt and Diana Waldfogel. San Francisco: Jossey-Bass, 1983.

Minehan, Thomas. *Boy and Girl Tramps of America*. New York: Farrar and Rinehart, 1934.

Nylander, Towne. "The Migrant Population of the United States." *American Journal of Sociology* 30, no. 2 (1924): 129–53.

————. "Wandering Youth." *Sociology and Social Research* 17, no. 6 (1933): 560–68.

O'Connor, P. *Britain in the Sixties: Vagrancy*. Baltimore: Penguin Books, 1963.

Park, R. E. "Human Migration and the Marginal Man." *American Journal of Sociology* 33, no. 6 (1928): 881–93.

Paul, Rodman Wilson. *Mining Frontiers of the Far West: 1848–1880*. New York: Holt, Rinehart and Winston, 1963.

Perry, Charles. *The Haight-Ashbury*. New York: Random House, 1984.

Perry, Helen Swick. *The Human Be-In*. New York: Basic Books, 1970.

Pittel, Stephen. *The Current Status of the Haight-Ashbury Hippie Community*. Unpublished manuscript, Wright Institute, Berkeley, 1968.

Pittel, S., and H. Miller. *Dropping Down*. Unpublished monograph, Wright Institute, Berkeley, 1968.

Potter, E. C. "The Problem of the Transient." *The Annals of the American Academy of Political and Social Science* 175 (November 1934): 66–73.

"Reagan on Homelessness: Many Choose to Live in the Streets." *New York Times*, 23 December 1988.

Reitman, B. L., ed. *Sister of the Road: The Autobiography of Boxcar Bertha*. New York: Harper and Row, 1937.

Report of the Working Party on Vagrancy and Street Offenses. London: Her Majesty's Stationery Office, 1976.

Ribton-Turner, C. J. *A History of Vagrants and Vagrancy*. Montclair, N.J.: Patterson Smith, 1972.

Riis, Jacob A. *How the Other Half Lives: Studies among the Tenements of New York*. 1890. Reprint. New York: Hill and Wang, 1957.

Robert Beale Burnside Projects, Inc. *A Survey of Persons Who Use Social Services on Skid Row*. Portland, Ore.: Author, 1973.

Robertson, Marjorie. "Homeless Veterans, an Emerging Problem." In *The Homeless in Contemporary Society*, edited by R. D. Bingham, R. E. Green, and S. B. White. Newbury Park, Calif.: Sage, 1987.

Ropers, R. H. *The Invisible Homeless: A New Urban Ecology*. New York: Human Sciences Press, 1988.

Rorty, James. "Counting the Homeless." *Nation*, 21 June 1933.

Rossi, Peter H., Gene A. Fisher, and Georgianna Willis. *The Condition of the Homeless of Chicago*. Report of the Social and Demographic Research Institute, University of Massachusetts, Amherst, and NORC, Social Science Research Center, University of Chicago, 1986.

Roucek, J. S. "The Tramping Movement in Central Europe." *Sociology and Social Research* 18, no. 2 (1933): 158–63.

Rubin, Jerry. *Do It! Scenarios of the Revolution*. New York: Simon and Schuster, 1970.

Sackville, R. *Homeless People and the Law*. Report by the Commissioner for Law and Poverty. Canberra, Australia: Australian Government Publishing Service, 1976.

Schneider, David M. "Transient Youth in This Century and the Last," *Jewish Social Service Quarterly* 9, no. 3 (June 1933): 305–9.

Shannon, David A. *The Great Depression.* Englewood Cliffs, N. J.: Prentice-Hall, 1960.

Skinner, M., and A. S. Nutt. "Adolescents Away from Home." *Annals of the American Academy of Political and Social Science* 236 (November 1944): 51–59.

Snow, D. A., S. G. Baker, and L. Anderson. "The Myth of Pervasive Mental Illness among the Homeless." *Social Problems* 33, no. 5 (1986): 407–23.

Solenberger, Alice W. *One Thousand Homeless Men: A Study of Original Records.* New York: Russell Sage Foundation, 1911.

Spradley, J. P. *You Owe Yourself a Drunk: An Ethnography of Urban Nomads.* Boston: Little, Brown, 1970.

Stefl, Mary E. "The New Homeless." *The Homeless in Contemporary Society,* edited by R. Bingham, R. Green, and S. White. Newbury Park, Calif.: Sage, 1987.

Stephenson, C. *An Analysis of Social Policy: Vagrancy.* Unpublished student paper, School of Social Welfare, University of California, Berkeley, 1968.

Stewart, J. *Of No Fixed Abode: Vagrancy and the Welfare State.* Manchester, England: Manchester University Press, 1975.

Surber, R. W., E. Dwyer, K. J. Ryan, S. M. Goldfinger, and J. T. Kelly. "Medical and Psychiatric Needs of the Homeless—A Preliminary Response." *Social Work* 33, no. 2 (1988): 116–19.

Terkel, Studs. *Hard Times: The Oral History of the Great Depression.* New York: Random House, 1970.

Thomas, D. B., ed. *The Book of Vagabonds and Beggars.* London: Penguin Press, 1932.

Thompson, E. P. *The Making of the English Working Class.* New York: Random House, 1963.

Timms, Noel. *Rootless in the City.* London: Bedford Square Press of the National Council of Social Service, 1968.

Trattner, Walter I. *From Poor Law to Welfare State.* New York: Free Press, 1974.

Travelers Aid Society. *Annual Statistical Report on Travelers Aid Services.* New York: Travelers Aid Society, 1974, 1975.

Trevelyan, G. M. *History of England.* 3 vols. London: Longmans, Green, 1934.

Tucker, W. "Where Do the Homeless Come From?" *National Review,* September 1987.

"Two Hundred Thousand Wandering Boys." *Fortune,* February 1933.

U.S. Bureau of the Census. *Poverty in the United States.* Current Population Reports, Series P–160, no. 163. Washington, D.C.: U.S. Government Printing Office, 1987.

U.S. Department of Housing and Urban Development, Office of Policy Development and Research. *A Report to the Secretary on the Homeless and Emergency Shelters.* Washington, D.C.: U.S. Government Printing Office, 1984.

Vexliard, A. *Introduction à la sociologie du vagabondage.* Paris: Librarie M. Riviere, 1956.

Vinograd, Julia. "Downhill." *Berkeley Street Cannibals.* Berkeley, Calif.: Oyez, 1976.

Wallace, Samuel E. *Skid Row as a Way of Life.* Totowa, N.J.: Bedminster Press, 1965.

Webb, J. N. *The Transient Unemployed.* Works Progress Administration Research Monograph no. 3. Washington, D.C.: U.S. Government Printing Office, 1938.

Webb, John N., and Malcolm Brown. *Migrant Families.* Works Progress Administration Research Monograph no. 18. Washington, D.C.: U.S. Government Printing Office, 1935.

Whiting, F. V. "Trespassers Killed on Railways." *Scientific American Supplement,* no. 1897 (1912): 303–4.

Wilhite, J. *Homelessness and Social Welfare in the United States: Prototypes of Reform, 1873–1987.* Ph.D. diss., University of California at Berkeley, 1989.

Whitman, W. *Leaves of Grass.* New York: University Press, 1965.

Wright, J. D. *Address Unknown: The Homeless in America.* New York: Aldine de Gruyter, 1989.

Ziegler, Phillip. *The Black Death.* Middlesex, England: Penguin Books, 1969.

Index

About the Author

Henry Miller was born and raised in a small town in New England during the depths of the Great Depression. After a short stint in the army, he received his bachelor's degree from Boston University and then earned a master's degree in social welfare from that same university. After receiving a doctorate from Columbia University in 1962, he joined the faculty at the University of California, Berkeley, where he is currently a professor in the School of Social Welfare.

He is the author of several books, monographs, and papers, including *Clinical and Social Judgment* (with James Bieri), *Problems and Issues in Social Casework* (with Scott Briar), and *An Introduction to Social Work Practice* (with Neil Gilbert and Harry Specht).